Ultimate
Business
Library

the Ultimate Business Library

50

books
that made
Management

Stuart Crainer

foreword and commentary by **Gary Hamel**

CAPSTONE

First published 1997 by
Capstone Publishing Limited
Oxford Centre for Innovation
Mill Street
Oxford OX2 0JX
United Kingdom

Reprinted 1997

British Library Cataloguing in Publication Data
A CIP catalogue record for this book is available from the British Library

ISBN 0-900961-02-4

Typeset in 11/14pt Plantin by
DP Photosetting, Aylesbury, Bucks
Printed and bound in Great Britain by
T.J. International Ltd, Padstow, Cornwall

This book is printed on acid-free paper

"There are no answers. Just, at best, a few guesses that might be worth a try."
Tom Peters

That's a brilliant idea. But how could it possibly work in my organization?

How often do you think as you read a business book that if only you could ask the author a simple question you could transform your organization?

Capstone is creating a unique partnership between authors and readers, delivering for the first time in business book publishing a genuine after-sales service for book buyers. Simply visit Capstone's home page on **http://www.bookshop.co.uk/capstone/** to leave your question (with details of date and place of purchase of a copy of *The Ultimate Business Library*) and Stuart Crainer will try to answer it.

Capstone authors travel and consult extensively so we do not promise 24-hour turnaround. But that one question answered might just jump start your company and your career.

Capstone is more than a publisher. It is an electronic clearing house for pioneering business thinking, putting the creators of new business ideas in touch with the people who use them.

CONTENTS

FOREWORD
Gary Hamel

To be both timely and timeless is a neat trick – one that is accomplished by all the books summarized in this volume. Each was very much a product of its times, and spoke to those times, but each has also stood the test of time. Managers have gone back to them again and again to rediscover enduring management truths.

As one scans this compendium, it is possible to catch glimpses of the transcendent issues that have occupied managers and management scholars down through the ages. Even more than the volumes contained herein, it is these issues which form the enduring bedrock of management practice and theory. And what might these issues be?

Management

What does it mean to be a manager? What are the roles and capabilities that distinguish "managers" from others in the organization?

With ever flatter organizations, and the emergence of small, self-organizing teams, the distinction between "management" and "labor" has become ever more blurred. Yet the fact that there is, today, a managerial component to almost every job increases rather than diminishes the need to be adept at organizing, integrating and coordinating – responsibilities traditionally associated with "management." Today we must speak of managing, rather than management. Nevertheless, anyone with a managerial role has much to learn from:

Barnard: *The Functions of the Executive*
Parker Follet: *Dynamic Administration*
Fayol: *General and Industrial Management*
Carnegie: *How to Win Friends and Influence People*
Drucker: *The Practice of Management*
Mintzberg: *The Nature of Managerial Work*
Semler: *Maverick*

Leadership

What is the distinction between management and leadership? What does it take to lead? Are leaders born or made? Can everyone aspire to be a leader?

There is, of course, a crucial distinction between management and leadership, between administrators and builders. A frequent lament is that many organizations are over-managed and under-led. The story of business is the story of great leaders. While the technology of management is highly developed (reporting, budgeting, controlling, reviewing, etc.), our understanding of leadership is more fuzzy. Leadership is not so much about *what* you do, but *how* you do it. Enumerating the attributes of leaders is relatively simple; turning bureaucrats into leaders is a rather more daunting task. This is the reason not everyone can be a Henry Ford, Tom Watson or Bill Gates. Nevertheless, the aspiring leader will find inspiration and guidance in:

Machiavelli: *The Prince*
Ford: *My Life and Work*
Burns: *Leadership*
Bennis & Nanus: *Leaders*
Watson: *A Business and Its Beliefs*

Complexity

What is the logic of the corporation? What are its boundaries? What are the advantages and disadvantages of size and complexity? Must scale and flexibility be mutually exclusive?

The greatest invention of modern times is not the electric light bulb, nor the telephone, nor the microprocessor, it is not even the general theory of relativity, the structure of DNA or quantum physics. It is, instead, the modern, large-scale industrial enterprise. It is this invention which, more than anything else, has brought unimagined prosperity to an ever-growing percentage of the world's inhabitants. Small may be beautiful, but big has its benefits. Despite the hype over virtual enterprises and network companies, the multidivisional, multinational company is here to stay. Look at a Johnson & Johnson, 3M or Citibank. The complexity of the modern corporation is mind-boggling. There are certainly costs to complexity, but our ability to minimize those costs, while maximizing the benefits of scale and scope has, in the last 150 years, produced an economic bonanza of unprecedented proportions. Just how has this been accomplished? Funny you should ask:

Weber: *The Theory of Social and Economic Organization*
Sloan: *My Years with General Motors*
Chandler: *Strategy and Structure*
Goold, Alexander & Campbell: *Corporate-Level Strategy*

People

Do people serve the organization, or is it the other way around? Can human beings be trusted at work, or must they be controlled? Can a job ever be more than a job?

An acquaintance of mine once remarked, "The thing you have to remember about organizations is that they're people, all the way down." This is something it's easy to forget in an increasingly technocratic, de-personalized world. Organizations are, more than anything else, social systems – with the emphasis on *social*. You may remember the old saw, "While with communism man exploited man, with capitalism it's the other way around." Despite the de-humanizing and debilitating effects of down-sizing and reengineering, we are finally coming to grips with the fact that (1) people really *are* a company's most valuable resource, (2) wealth really does derive more from the accumulation of knowledge capital than from the accumulation of physical capital, (3) every employee really does have a brain, and (4) in an indeterminate world, where command-and-control is simply not possible, employees really must be trusted to do the right thing. Enlightenment has been a long time coming. That it has dawned at all owes much to the work of:

Belbin: *Management Teams*
Herzberg: *The Motivation to Work*
McGregor: *The Human Side of Enterprise*
Maslow: *Motivation and Personality*

Customers

What do customers really want? What are the foundations of customer loyalty? What does it mean to be market-led? How can a company consistently exceed customer expectations?

Socialism is dead. If you listen carefully, you can hear its death rattle in some of Europe's more sclerotic economies. In China communism is nothing more than an ideological veneer on nearly unbridled capitalism. Around the world Adam Smith's "invisible hand" is hard at work improving the lot of consumers everywhere. We should all be grateful: in a market economy, the invisible hand punishes any company that fails to worship at the altar of our needs. The purpose of organizations, whether public or private is, after all, to satisfy the customer. This was a fact implicitly understood by Deming and Juran. The debt customers owe these two quality "gurus" is only slightly smaller than that they owe Adam Smith himself. Yet many companies have only recently got the customer religion. Not so long ago IBM celebrated "The Year of the Customer." One wonders what the company celebrated in other years – "The Year of the Monkey," perhaps? While Adam Smith laid the philosophical foundations for the market economy, Professors Kotler and Levitt have helped thousands of companies become truly market-facing. If you, or someone you know, needs reminding that the market is the final arbiter of organizational success, you'd do well to turn to:

Smith: *The Wealth of Nations*
Deming: *Out of the Crisis*
Juran: *Juran on Planning for Quality*
Kotler: *Marketing Management*
Levitt: *Innovation in Marketing*

Global

What does it mean to be global? Must a company be global? How does one build cohesion in a global enterprise? When should one respect local differences? When should one ignore local differences?

Business has been global since the dawn of the industrial age. (Remember the East India Company?) Companies like Ford,

IBM, Shell, Unilever and Nestlé have long thought of themselves as citizens of the world. But it's only in recent years that they've recognized they must become truly global. Converging customer needs, political integration, global media, and the economies of global scale cannot be ignored. The tide of globalization cannot be reversed. Of course, enterprise itself has been at the forefront of the globalization trend – companies are taking capital, technology and management skills into even the most isolated economies. Interdependence is inevitable. Countries that a decade ago regarded the multinational with enmity today recognize that to eschew the multinational is to eschew economic development itself. By the way, one of the things it means to be global is to be willing and able to learn from different management cultures. Western companies have learned much from their Asian competitors over the past few years – about quality, supplier management, mass customization, and accelerated product development. Parochialism and arrogance are dangerous in the global economy. If you're still wondering just what it means to be global, you'll find answers in:

Porter: *The Competitive Advantage of Nations*
Bartlett and Ghoshal: *Managing Across Borders*
Ohmae: *The Borderless World*
Pascale & Athos: *The Art of Japanese Management*
Trompenaars: *Riding the Waves of Culture*

The Future

How will our world be different in the future? How is the context of management changing? Can we know the future? Can we prepare for it?

Some managers, and indeed some companies, seem more prescient than others – they seem to live deeply in the future. They can almost smell the winds of change. They act while others react. Now, I don't think anyone out there has a crystal ball. If God reveals the future to anyone, it's not to the chairmen/women of *Fortune* 500 companies. There are some, though, who possess great peripheral vision – they see things that are already happening, but have not yet entered main-stream consciousness. As William Gibson, the author of *Neuromancer*, so aptly put it, "The future's already happened, it's just unequally distributed." So here's a piece of advice, if you want to see the future coming, look where others aren't. Drucker, Handy and Toffler have each, in their own time, pointed our attention to an inflection point that distinguishes the future from the past. Hamel and Prahalad tell you how to find the future. If you want proof that a wide angle lens can help you get to the future first, you'll find it in the pages of:

> Drucker: *The Age of Discontinuity*
> Handy: *The Age of Unreason*
> Toffler: *The Third Wave*
> Hamel & Prahalad: *Competing for the Future*

Renewal

What are the secrets of continued organizational vitality? Why do some companies thrive on change, while others are destroyed by change? Is it possible to revector and redirect the energies of a large industrial enterprise?

Perhaps the single biggest challenge for any enterprise, of any size, is to maintain its relevancy in a topsy-turvy world. Never has the gap between old solutions and new problems been greater. Never have so many companies been so out of synch with the environment in which they find themselves. This should not be surprising – the future happens faster than it used to. So "organizational change" has become a growth business for management gurus and consultants. But the "vitality problem," as I like to term it, can be addressed at two levels: (1) How to revitalize moribund companies; and (2) how to preserve vitality in currently successful companies. I think the second question is far more interesting than the first. What I would wish for you, dear reader, is that you never have to live through a dramatic "turn-around," just as I would wish that you never have to confront and overcome a life-threatening illness. Much better not to get sick in the first place. One can find more than an ounce of prevention in:

Kanter: *The Change Masters*
Peters & Waterman: *In Search of Excellence* (a call to renewal)
Pascale: *Managing on the Edge*
Peters: *Liberation Management*
Schein: *Organizational Culture and Leadership*
Argyris & Schon: *Organizational Learning*
Senge: *The Fifth Discipline*

Competition

How does one create lasting competitive advantage? What are the strategies for winning in a contested marketplace? How does one capture a disproportionate share of the profits in an industry or industry segment?

A recent book was optimistically titled *The End of Competition*. It didn't make it into this volume. For while new, collaborative forms of industrial organization are rampant, the fact is that the marketplace remains a brutal, Darwinian sort of place. Sure, companies are collaborating, but even as they collaborate they compete to get at each other's skills, to maximize their share of the spoils, and to direct the partnership to their own particular ends. If war is diplomacy by other means, collaboration is competition by other means. In a world of scarce resources, competition will always be endemic, whether among microbes or multinational companies. Competition is as old as humankind itself – from the first fist that was thrown over a property dispute, to sophisticated battles over patent rights. Of course the goal of competition is always the same – to occupy the high ground, be it battlements on a hill, or the operating system for the personal computer. So fight we must. And few can better tell you how than:

Sun-Tzu: *The Art of War*
Porter: *Competitive Strategy*

Efficiency

How can we do more with less? How can we maximize the ratio of output over input? How can we become the world's lowest cost producer?

In a global economy, there is simply no place for inefficiency to hide. Much, though certainly not all, of competition is focused on driving costs to zero. You have to believe that Frederick Winslow Taylor would have loved Wal-Mart, Sony, or Federal Express – modern icons of efficiency. Champy and Hammer have been equally fervent apostles of corporate efficiency. Over the coming decades, the world will become even less tolerant of inefficiency. With on-line shopping and digital commerce, customers will have perfect price information. Indeed, we can expect customers to put more and more of their purchases out to bid: "Here's what I want this week, now who's going to bring it to me at the lowest possible cost?" Yet the goal is not simply cost minimization, it's value maximization. Any company that competes only on cost, and can't offer its customers unique benefits, will find it difficult, if not impossible, to make money. No customer buys solely on the basis of cost – something America's discount airlines learned to their sorrow when customers deserted them over safety fears. But if it's cutting that turns you on, you'll find substantial excitement in the pages of:

Taylor: *Scientific Management*
Champy & Hammer: *Reengineering the Corporation*

Strategy

Where are we heading? What is our destiny? What is it that unites us? What are we trying to build? Where and how can we win?

These are the questions that concern the strategist. Yet answers are difficult to come by. Traditional strategic planning has been discredited. As Henry Mintzberg argues so well, planning creates plans, it doesn't create strategy. This is the dirty little secret at the heart of the strategy industry. For while we all know a brilliant strategy when we see one, we don't know where great strategies come from. We have built an entire strategy edifice (planning, consulting companies, MBA courses) without a theory of strategy creation! Maybe the best advice that could be given is to wait until 11.00pm, eat a fiery hot Vindaloo curry, and hope that you get struck with a strategy insight at 3.00 in the morning. Well, maybe we can do a little better than that. So while Ansoff and Mintzberg tilt at each other's windmills, I would recommend the reader to thoughtful volumes by Ohmae, and (once again) Hamel and Prahalad – for here can be found the antecedents of strategy. Nevertheless, read on:

Ansoff: *Corporate Strategy*
Mintzberg: *The Rise and Fall of Strategic Planning*
Ohame: *The Mind of the Strategist*
Hamel & Prahalad: *Competing for the Future*

Fun

*Does corporate life have to be dreary? Do we have to take ourselves
so seriously? Do vice presidents have to be dull? If it ain't fun, is it
worth it?*

Let's lighten up here! When was the last time work gave you a
good belly *laugh*, rather than a belly*ful*? I probably shouldn't
mention it, but the best-selling business book of all time
didn't even make our top 50 list. As I'm writing this, *The
Dilbert Principle* is selling at the rate of 50,000 copies a week.
This irreverent and acidly witty collection of cartoons and
management *bon mots* has even outsold that beacon of hope,
In Search of Excellence. Hope is good, funny is better. Here's a
sample, one that skewers a concept near and dear to me. Mr.
Manager asks Dogbert, the consultant, "So just what is our
core competence?" "You'll be pleased to know that your core
competence is paying money to consultants," Dogbert replies
nonchalantly. "But surely, that can't be the only thing we're
good at," protests Mr. Manager. "Well," frowns Dogbert, "I
guess we could count whining!" Well, you couldn't expect us
to include a book of cartoons in this volume now, could you?
A full-throated belly laugh is just too much of a good thing.
On the other hand, you'll get a wry smile from reading:

Parkinson: *Parkinson's Law*
Townsend: *Up the Organization*

So there it is. Fifty books and several hundred years of
managerial wisdom. At the rate of a book a week you could
plow through this list and still have a Christmas holiday.
Happy reading!

Prof. Gary Hamel
Chairman, Strategos
Visiting Professor, The London Business School
November 1996

PREFACE
The Ultimate Business
Library

The Ultimate Business Library is an objective selection of books. Views on the selection were canvassed on both sides of the Atlantic. Some contain the germ of a great idea; others are brimming with genius. Some were highly influential despite obvious deficiencies; others were commercial failures yet contain ideas which have proved enduringly important and practically useful.

Of course, any selection excludes some books which could – sometimes should – have been included. To ease our consciences, the appendix lists a further fifty books, each with a short summary. The fifty books selected in *The Ultimate Business Library* and its appendix are, for ease of reference, arranged by author in alphabetical order.

Looking at the list of titles, it is notable that few of the books are written by practicing managers or by women. Books by actual managers largely provide proof of why the individuals chose a career in business rather than in the media. They tend to be riddled with egotism and poor writing. Our selection includes a mere handful by practitioners (Chester Barnard, Alfred P. Sloan, Thomas Watson, Henry Ford, Henri Fayol, Robert Townsend and Ricardo Semler). The vast majority are written by academics from the leading US business schools.

Critics of business books would suggest that therein lies the problem. Academics and consultants are routinely condemned as being out of touch with business reality. In some cases this is undoubtedly true. But, the broad ranging perspectives and research which goes into many of these works means that they are required reading. The individual experiences of a single executive in a particular organization are unlikely to provide a rich vein of inspiration for executives in wildly different situations.

The lack of women writers is a reflection of traditional prejudices. Even now, books on management and business are largely written by – and for – men. There are a few exceptions. Rosabeth Moss Kanter plows a lonely furrow as the leading female managerial thinker of our time. Few other women have succeeded in shaping management – in the early part of the century, Harvard's Mary Parker Follett had a career of unsung brilliance which only now is gaining wider recognition.

There are drawbacks, prejudices, and deficiencies in any selection. But the fifty books celebrated in *The Ultimate Business Library* have unquestionably had profound effects on managers and organizations throughout the world. And, as is now being realized, what affects the business world affects us all.

Stuart Crainer
November 1996

ABOUT THE AUTHORS

Stuart Crainer is a writer and editor. He is the author of *The Future of Leadership* (with Randall P. White & Philip Hodgson); *The Real Power of Brands; Making Re-engineering Happen* (with Eddie Obeng); and *Key Management Ideas*. He is the editor of the *Financial Times Handbook of Management* and his biography of Tom Peters will be published by Capstone in 1997.

Gary Hamel is Visiting Professor of Strategic and International Management at London Business School and co-author of the best-selling *Competing for the Future*. He is Chairman of Strategos, a worldwide strategic consulting company based in California.

ACKNOWLEDGEMENTS

Mark Allin of Capstone Publishing came up with the idea of *The Ultimate Business Library*. It was so simple that I thought it must have been done before. But, as business people often discover, simple ideas are often the most elusive.

I am also indebted to Liza Jones and the staff of Henley Management College. They generously allowed me access to their excellent facilities and use of their library.

The selection of books was tested out on a variety of people in the UK and US. Their opinions and input were extremely useful in honing the list down. Any omissions, however, are the responsibility of the author.

Grateful acknowledgements is made to the *Harvard Business Review* for permission to use the following extracts from:

'Teaching smart people how to learn' by Chris Argyris, *Harvard Business Review*, May–June 1991 © 1991 Copyright the President and Fellows of Harvard College; all rights reserved.

'Reengineering work: don't automate, obliterate' by Michael Hammer, *Harvard Business Review*, July–August 1990 © 1990 Copyright the President and Fellows of Harvard College; all rights reserved.

'Marketing myopia' by Ted Levitt, *Harvard Business Review*, July–August 1960 © 1960 Copyright the

INTRODUCTION

The Ultimate Business Library is a collection of fifty of the greatest books of management. Each book is summarized together with a biography of the author and a commentary by Gary Hamel. The intention is to whet your appetite and encourage you to seek out the originals (though this is not easy in many cases). *The Ultimate Business Library* will also enable you to update your knowledge on an individual thinker's major ideas and areas of expertise.

To assemble fifty of the greatest books written on management twenty years ago would have been a straightforward task. The only problem might have been in finding fifty. Times change. The last two decades have seen an explosion of interest in business and management books. They routinely feature in bestseller lists, arouse controversy and earn some of their authors large amounts of money. Along the way, usually through a process of osmosis rather than dramatic conversion, they also alter the ways in which managers manage.

In the instant, action-oriented, pressurized world of business, books change things. They change perceptions. They change behavior. They alter expectations and aspirations. In no other field do books now hold such a central role in the dissemination of best practice and new concepts. Helped by the fact that business is increasingly global and the skills of management often universal, books make their way round the world, shaping the management of the future.

Of course, books do not necessarily change things for the better. One author's interpretation of the future is not necessarily the right future for you or your organization. In spite of all the books, most executives are not great managers of their own time who hatch perfect corporate strategies in empowered teams. Nor do they work in virtual organizations harnessing the latest in technology. Ideas and our interpretations of ideas are rarely identical. And many of the ideas are best ignored.

Look at the wave of enthusiasm for reengineering which dominated the business book market at the beginning of the 1990s. Opinions differ on whether reengineering is the route to corporate nirvana or an overblown waste of corporate time and energy. But, whatever your opinion, there can be no doubting the effect reengineering has had. At the height of reengineering's popularity, a study of 624 companies by CSC Index (*The State of Reengineering*) found that 75 percent of European companies had at least one reengineering project in progress and half of those which did not were planning to have one in the near future.

James Champy who, with Michael Hammer, has popularized the concept, estimated in 1993 that 50 percent of large US companies were claiming to be in the process of reengineering.[1] Many have – and will – find reengineering impractical, but that does not negate its influence and the changes of perception, behavior and practice it has instigated. Negative experiences are still experiences. (In the case of reengineering, James Champy estimates that over two-thirds of initiatives fail to meet expectations. A recent study showed only one company in ten achieving breakthroughs in performance and reported that most completed projects 'achieved only modest improvements'.[2])

This flurry of activity largely stems from Champy and Hammer's bestselling *Reengineering the Corporation* (1993), a book which seized managerial imaginations in a way that a succession of books have done over recent years. The book which ignited the business book market was undoubtedly *In Search of Excellence* written by two McKinsey and Company consultants, Thomas J. Peters and Robert H. Waterman. Its publication in October 1982 marked a watershed in business book publishing and, some would say, in management.

In Search of Excellence has now sold around six million copies. Its success, however, took everyone by surprise – no one more so than its two authors. Prior to publication Peters and Waterman actually distributed 15,000 photocopies of the book to interested parties. Their publishers were appalled. It seemed as if the duo had given away many more copies than they were likely to sell. When the book appeared, to often lukewarm reviews, a groundswell began. The 15,000 free copies proved a piece of fortuitously brilliant marketing – the recipients were so impressed (or grateful) that they rushed out to buy their copy. The book took off in a way neither had expected or previously experienced. Before long the Basking Ridge book store in New Jersey near AT&T headquarters was selling 2,000 copies a week.

Thanks to the book's success, Thomas J. Peters has now been transformed into the folksy and friendly Tom Peters, multimillionaire, globe-trotting guru, the ultimate beneficiary of the business book boom – and, lest it be forgotten, its instigator. ('We should all be grateful to Tom,' one business writer told me.) After *In Search of Excellence* stormed into the bestseller lists, others quickly followed. Before long business books were everywhere. Airport book stalls confined the Harold Robbins blockbusters to a distant corner and filled their shelves with the latest outpourings from the array of consultants, academics, journalists, retired executives, charlatans and scribblers anxious to join the bandwagon.

The New Knowledge Imperative

Whether *In Search of Excellence* was a good book or not continues to be debated. But, its influence is undeniable. More broadly, the sudden and unexpected growth in management books can be attributed to a number of other factors. Since 1945 we have witnessed the inexorable 'professionalization' of management (indeed, some have argued that we have witnessed the professionalization of almost every occupation). Instead of being a slightly grubby and seedy profession, management has become accepted as an honorable and potentially lucrative means of earning a living. Managers were once mere supervisors, small-time dictators; now, they are executives, globe-trotting, intelligent, highly qualified, forging their own role.

Professionals they may be, but managers remain slightly reticent and ill-at-ease with the nobleness of their profession. They feel a need to explain themselves in a way in which lawyers or doctors do not. They are professionals, but where is the kudos? After all, young children do not express strong urges to become chief executives – and those that do are more likely to be taken to child psychologists than to witness their first production line in operation.

Managers frequently explain themselves with their business cards and their job titles. They explain themselves through their company cars and the stunning variety of executive perks. And they seek legitimacy through the acquisition of knowledge.

Managers crave a clear set of guidelines on the skills and knowledge required to become a manager. If theirs is a profession, they would like professional qualifications. There is a perennial and largely futile debate about the mythical 'chartered manager' – as if a single qualification could equip an executive to manage a steel producer in Illinois, a chain of shoe stores in Spain or a wine importing business in Auckland, New Zealand.

In the past, the quest for knowledge – new tools, techniques and ideas – was part of the process of professionalization. Now, it is the route to survival.

If knowledge means survival, managers cannot and should

not be criticized for their relentless search for new skills and new approaches. But, too often these resemble an indecent race to find the latest bright idea, the single-stop answer to all their business problems. Managers are addicted to the newest and brightest ideas. They buy the fashionable books of the moment and then within months, perhaps weeks, move on to the next fashion. This is good news for publishers.

For managers it means a relentless and largely impossible quest to keep up to date with the latest thinking. Books and articles are devoured and pored over. It is a losing battle, but one they must endeavor to fight – 'The only thing worse than slavishly following management theory is ignoring it completely,' observed *The Economist* (February 26, 1994).

Richard Pascale, author of *Managing on the Edge*, is a vehement critic of the managerial enthusiasm for fads and instant solutions. In *Managing on the Edge* he charts the rise and rise of fads since the 1950s. He calculates that over two dozen techniques have come and gone during this period – with a dozen arriving between 1985 and 1990 alone. Pascale believes that this trend is likely to continue. 'I think it is a packaged goods business. There is an unquenchable thirst,' he says. 'If you take the premise, as I do, that corporations are the dominant social institutions of our age, you have to reckon with the fact that corporations are very influential. Certain trappings go with the party. It is part of the fanfare surrounding these institutions. With that comes a constant churn of material for corporate chieftains to feed on. Because of their prominence in society this is always going to be with us, though among the CEOs I speak to, there is a certain cynicism about the material.'[3]

Rodney Turner of the UK's Henley Management College believes there is a range of responses to what the management thinkers say. 'There are those who ignore the gurus completely and pig-headedly refuse to change the way they manage. They learnt management in the university of life and have no time for "book learning". At the other extreme are the sycophants who slavishly follow what the gurus say and often apply their ideas unquestioningly and inappropriately and usually make a mess of it,' observes Turner. 'In the middle there are those who read what the gurus have to say, pick out some good ideas, adapt them to their environment and make them work. But some of what the gurus say they take with a pinch of salt and they also realize that there is no philosopher's stone that turns lead to gold in all circumstances and hence everything must be adapted.'[4]

The truth is that, despite the hype and the relentless stream of fads, the great ideas of management have been around for a while – indeed, some would say that the basics of management have existed since time immemorial. Ideas which purport to be bright and new are often colorful imitations of age old concepts of hackneyed reworkings. (Indeed, if you wanted to identify the first business blockbuster you would have to go back to 1832 when Charles Babbage's *On the Economy of Machinery and Manufactures* reputedly sold 10,000 copies.)

And, much of what is written is indigestible. Economist John Kay describes the formula for an article in the *Harvard Business Review*: 'One idea per article, although it will not be taken seriously if expressed in less than 3,000 words. Assume no prior knowledge of anything ... definitely no jokes – our audience has no sense of humor – but frequent references to exchanges with senior executives such as John Harvey-Jones and Akio Morita.'[5]

Business and management writing is continually subject to such barbs. Better than anyone, managers know that quantity does not equate with quality. There are a lot of poor management books – laden with jargon, fashionable phrases, and smart retrospective case studies. It is easy to forget that the same applies to the literature of any profession. Not all law books are authoritative – many are unreadable, and as bogged down in jargon as the worst managerial text.

Expectations of management books are extraordinarily high. A manager in Rutland, Vermont, reads a book by a

French academic filled with case studies of Swiss-Swedish conglomerates and expects answers to his or her problems.

The skeptics are right to question the practical usefulness of much that is published. 'You can be very bold as a theoretician. Good theories are like good art. A practitioner has to compromise,' says Warren Bennis.[6] Even so, the canon of management literature is full of ideas which have been implemented and which have affected the lives and performance of millions of managers. 'All the great business builders we know of – from the Medici of Renaissance Florence and the founders of the Bank of England in the late seventeenth century down to IBM's Thomas Watson in our day – had a clear theory of the business which informed all their actions and decisions,' observes Peter Drucker in *Management.* Cut through the dross and there is a broad swathe of carefully researched, well-written, insightful books on what makes managers and their organizations tick.

The *Harvard Business Review* may be lacking in humor and brevity, but a great deal of the material it includes is perceptive and practically useful. There are business books which stand the tests of time and usefulness. They are not placebos, but vibrant cures.

And, lest it be forgotten, books and the research behind them, do change things. Look at the part played by W. Edwards Deming in the renaissance of Japan. Think of the impact of Michael Porter's work on the value chain which has been taken up by companies throughout the world, as well as his work on national competitiveness which has altered the economic perspectives of entire countries. Porter has been called in by countries as far apart as Portugal and Colombia to shed light on their competitiveness. Who thought customer service was a key competitive weapon before Peters and Waterman? In the business world, books are more than ornamental shelf-fillers.

And their domain is growing. On his election to become leader of the House of Representatives, Newt Gingrich sent his Republican colleagues an essential reading list. It included works by seven management thinkers. In 1993, President Clinton established the National Performance Review and has backed the creation of a public sector MBA. The influence of best management practice and leading-edge thinking is increasingly all pervasive.

Notes

1 Quoted by Christopher Lorenz in 'Uphill struggle to become horizontal', *Financial Times*, November 5, 1993.
2 This study, entitled *Re-engineering: The Critical Success Factors*, was carried out by Business Intelligence, London, 1995.
3 Interview with Stuart Crainer, July 23, 1996.
4 Correspondence with author, November 9, 1995.
5 John Kay, 'Handy guide to corporate life, *Financial Times*, August 17, 1995.
6 Quoted by Stuart Crainer in 'Doing the right thing', *The Director*, October 1988.

FIFTY BOOKS WHICH MADE MANAGEMENT

MANAGERIAL PRE-HISTORY

Sun Tzu	*The Art of War*	(500 BC)
Nicolo Machiavelli	*The Prince*	(1513)
Adam Smith	*The Wealth of Nations*	(1776)

1900–1929

Frederick W. Taylor	*The Principles of Scientific Management*	(1911)
Henri Fayol	*General and Industrial Management*	(1916)
Henry Ford	*My Life and Work*	(1923)

THE THIRTIES

Dale Carnegie	*How to Win Friends and Influence People*	(1937)
Chester Barnard	*The Functions of the Executive*	(1938)

THE FORTIES

Mary Parker Follett	*Dynamic Administration*	(1941)
Max Weber	*Theory of Social and Economic Organization*	(1947)

THE FIFTIES

Abraham Maslow	*Motivation and Personality*	(1954)
Peter F. Drucker	*The Practice of Management*	(1954)
C.N. Parkinson	*Parkinson's Law*	(1958)
Frederick Herzberg	*The Motivation to Work*	(1959)

THE SIXTIES

Douglas McGregor	*The Human Side of Enterprise*	(1960)
Ted Levitt	*Innovation in Marketing*	(1962)
Alfred Chandler	*Strategy and Structure*	(1962)
Thomas Watson Jr.	*A Company and its Beliefs*	(1963)
Alfred P. Sloan	*My Years with General Motors*	(1963)
Igor Ansoff	*Corporate Strategy*	(1965)
Philip Kotler	*Marketing Management*	(1967)
Peter F. Drucker	*The Age of Discontinuity*	(1969)

THE SEVENTIES

Robert Townsend	*Up the Organization*	(1970)
Henry Mintzberg	*The Nature of Managerial Work*	(1973)
Chris Argyris & Donald Schon	*Organizational Learning*	(1978)
James MacGregor Burns	*Leadership*	(1978)

THE EIGHTIES

Michael Porter	*Competitive Strategy*	(1980)
Alvin Toffler	*The Third Wave*	(1980)
Richard Pascale & Anthony Athos	*The Art of Japanese Management*	(1981)
Tom Peters & Robert Waterman	*In Search of Excellence*	(1982)
Kenichi Ohmae	*The Mind of the Strategist*	(1982)
W. Edwards Deming	*Out of the Crisis*	(1982)

Rosabeth Moss Kanter	*Change Masters*	(1983)
Meredith Belbin	*Management Teams*	(1984)
Warren Bennis & Burt Nanus	*Leaders*	(1985)
Edgar Schein	*Organizational Culture and Leadership*	(1985)
Joseph M. Juran	*Juran on Planning for Quality*	(1985)
Christopher Bartlett & Sumantra Ghoshal	*Managing Across Borders*	(1989)
Charles Handy	*The Age of Unreason*	(1989)

THE NINETIES

Kenichi Ohmae	*The Borderless World*	(1990)
Michael Porter	*The Competitive Advantage of Nations*	(1990)
Richard Pascale	*Managing on the Edge*	(1990)
Peter Senge	*The Fifth Discipline*	(1990)
Tom Peters	*Liberation Management*	(1992)
Ricardo Semier	*Maverick!*	(1993)
James Champy & Michael Hammer	*Reengineering the Corporation*	(1993)
Fons Trompenaars	*Riding the Waves of Culture*	(1993)
Henry Mintzberg	*The Rise and Fall of Strategic Planning*	(1994)
Michael Goold, Andrew Campbell & Marcus Alexander	*Corporate-Level Strategy*	(1994)
Gary Hamel & C.K. Prahalad	*Competing for the Future*	(1994)

IGOR ANSOFF

Corporate Strategy

1965

IGOR ANSOFF

Igor Ansoff is Distinguished Professor of Strategic Management at the US International University in San Diego, President of Ansoff Associates and a member of the board of Gemini Consulting.

Born in Vladivostock in 1918, Ansoff trained as an engineer and mathematician. After leaving Brown University, he worked for the RAND Corporation and then the Lockheed Corporation where he was a Vice-President. In 1963 he left industry for academia, joining Carnegie-Mellon's Graduate School of Business Administration. He was then founding Dean and Professor of Management at Vanderbilt University's Graduate School of Management before becoming a Professor at the European Institute for Advanced Studies in Management in Belgium. Ansoff has also taught at the Stockholm School of Economics. He joined the US International University in 1983.

Corporate Strategy was Ansoff's first book. He has followed it with a number of unstintingly serious academic studies including *Strategic Management* (1979); and *Implanting Strategic Management* (2nd edition 1990). A revised version of *Corporate Strategy*, entitled *New Corporate Strategy*, was published in 1988.

gor Ansoff's *Corporate Strategy* is not an easy book to read. Indeed, to the reader of the 1990s used to a stream of exhortations and personal reminiscence, it frequently appears to be impenetrable and inaccessible. Yet, its influence was – and continues to be – significant.

Ansoff has explained its genesis (Ansoff, 1994): '*Corporate Strategy* integrated strategic planning concepts which were invented independently in a number of leading American firms, including Lockheed. It also presented several new theoretical concepts such as partial ignorance, business strategy, capability and competence profiles, and synergy. One particular concept, the product-mission matrix, became very popular, because it was simple and codified for the first time the differences between strategic expansion and diversification.'

The book's starting point was a vacation during which Ansoff grew a beard, consumed half a case of Scotch and contemplated strategy. In writing *Corporate Strategy*, Ansoff's aim was 'to codify and generalize' his experiences working at Lockheed. The book intends 'to develop a practically useful series of concepts and procedures which managers can use to manage … a practical method for strategic decision making within a business firm,' says Ansoff in his preface.

Corporate Strategy was timely – 'It was published at a time of widespread enthusiasm for strategic planning and an increasing number of firms were joining the ranks of its users,' recalls Ansoff (1994). Until *Corporate Strategy*, strategic planning was a barely understood, *ad hoc* concept. It was practiced, while the theory lay largely unexplored.

In *Corporate Strategy*, Ansoff provides a rational model by which strategic and planning decisions can be made. Ansoff looks at strategic, administrative and operating decisions. (The model concentrates on corporate expansion and diversification rather than strategic planning as a whole.) From this emerges the Ansoff Model of Strategic Planning, a complex sequence of decisions or, what Ansoff calls, a 'cascade of decisions, starting with highly aggregated ones and proceeding toward the more specific'.

Central to this cascade is the concept of gap analysis: see where you are; identify where you wish to be; and identify tasks which will take you there. Ansoff explains: 'The procedure within each step of the cascade is similar.

1 A set of objectives is established.
2 The difference (the "gap") between the current position of the firm and the objectives is estimated.
3 One or more courses of action (strategy) is proposed.
4 These are tested for their "gap-reducing properties". A course is accepted if it substantially closes the gap; if it does not, new alternatives are tried.'

Corporate Strategy is also notable for its introduction of the word 'synergy' to the management vocabulary. This has become overused, though Ansoff's explanation ('2 + 2 = 5') remains memorably simple. And, Ansoff also examines 'corporate advantage' long before Michael Porter's masterly dissection of the subject in the 1980s.

While *Corporate Strategy* was a remarkable book for its times, its flaws have been widely acknowledged – most honestly by Ansoff himself. *Corporate Strategy* is highly prescriptive and advocates heavy reliance on analysis. As a result, its adherents encountered, what Ansoff labeled, 'paralysis by analysis' – the more information they possessed, the more they thought they needed. This vicious circle dogged many organizations who embraced strategic planning with enthusiasm.

Strategic planning, as proposed in *Corporate Strategy*, provides more questions than answers. This was quickly acknowledged by Ansoff (1994) who regarded strategic planning as an 'incomplete invention' though 'on an intuitive level, I was convinced that strategic planning was an inherently useful management tool.' He has spent the last 30 years attempting to prove that this is the case and that, rather than being prescriptive and unwieldy, strategic management can be a dynamic tool able to cope with the unexpected twists of turbulent markets as well as the more secure times described in *Corporate Strategy*.

2

CHRIS ARGYRIS & DONALD SCHON

Organizational Learning: A Theory of Action Perspective

1978

Hamel on Argyris & Schon

"If your organization has not yet mastered double-loop learning it is already a dinosaur. No one can doubt that organizational learning is the ultimate competitive advantage. We owe much to Argyris and Schon for helping us learn about learning."

Chris Argyris & Donald Schon

Chris Argyris (born 1923) is the James B. Conant Professor at the Harvard Graduate Schools of Business and Education. Argyris is a formidable intellectual even by Harvard's lofty standards. Prior to joining Harvard in 1971 he was at Yale and his qualifications embrace psychology, economics and organizational behavior. His books include *Personality and Organization* (1957); *Overcoming Organizational Defenses* (1990); *On Organizational Learning*, (1993); and *Knowledge for Action* (1993).

Donald Schon (born 1930) was educated at Yale, the Sorbonne and Harvard University. After teaching philosophy at UCLA and the University of Kansas, he joined consultants Arthur D. Little in 1957 and later worked for the US Department of Commerce. He was then President of the Organization for Social and Technical Innovation at MIT where he also became Ford Professor of Urban Studies and Education. Schon pioneered the concept of 'action science', an investigative and intimate approach to dealing with problems and errors. (*Organizational Learning*'s sub-title is '*A theory of action perspective*'.) Schon gave the 1970 Reith Lectures for the BBC from which was born the book, *Beyond the Stable State* (1978).

Argyris and Schon also co-authored *Theory in Practice: Increasing Professional Efficiency* (1974).

L ean and ascetic of appearance, Chris Argyris' work is driven by a fundamental – some would say flawed – faith in human nature. His earlier work was well-received, but only as carefully argued academic studies; thoughtful and profound, but not necessarily the stuff of commercial reality.

In the last decade, the tides of change have swept Argyris' way. Suddenly his ideas are fashionable. This is most apparent in the upsurge of interest in the concept of the learning organization. Argyris and Schon's *Organizational Learning* appeared in 1978, but it took the 1990 bestseller from MIT's Peter Senge, *The Fifth Discipline*, to propel the learning organization from academic concept to mainstream acceptance. (Not, of course, that the world has instantly been transformed. Managers may agree with the idea, but are usually loathe to implement the learning organization's full ramifications.)

If you wished to trace the roots of the learning organization you would invariably find yourself reading Argyris and Schon's *Organizational Learning*.

Organizational Learning tackles the central paradoxes of business life. Such as how can individual initiative and creativity work in an organizational environment where rules will always exist and how can teamworking and individual working co-exist fruitfully. Argyris and Schon's partnership produces interesting perspectives on such perennial problems – Schon is more of a philosopher; Argyris a psychologist. *Organizational Learning* grew out of Argyris and Schon's 1974 book, *Theory in Practice*. 'Originally, we had planned in a chapter of that book to apply the theory of action perspective to the problem of organizational capacity for learning. But we could not write that chapter; it called for a conceptual bridge which we had not yet built – a bridge between the world of interpersonal behavior and the world of the organization,' write Argyris and Schon. 'In the present work, we argue that organizations are not collections of individuals which can be understood solely in terms of the social psychology of group behavior.'

Organizational Learning, therefore, acts as a theoretical bridge between a variety of disciplines. 'There is an urgent need for alternative visions of science, and Schon's work along with that of Argyris provides some of the best ideas and answers. Few have gone so far in reconciling the vigor of relevance and in building a bridge between the isolated academic fortresses of the sciences and the humanities,' says Charles Hampden-Turner of the University of Cambridge's Judge Institute of Management.

Argyris and Schon investigate two basic organizational models. Model 1 is based on the premise that we seek to manipulate and form the world in accordance with our individual aspirations and wishes. In Model 1 managers concentrate on establishing individual goals. They keep to themselves and do not voice concerns or disagreements. The onus is on creating a conspiracy of silence in which everyone dutifully keeps their head down. Defense is the prime activity in a Model 1 organization though occasionally the best means of defense is attack. Model 1 managers are prepared to inflict change on others, but resist any attempt to change their own thinking and working practices. Model 1 organizations are characterized by what Argyris and Schon label 'single-loop learning' ('when the detection and correction of organizational error permits the organization to carry on its present policies and achieve its current objectives').

In contrast, Model 2 organizations emphasize 'double-loop learning' which Argyris and Schon describe as 'when organizational error is detected and corrected in ways that involve the modification of underlying norms, policies, and objectives'. In Model 2 organizations, managers act on information; they debate issues and respond to, and are prepared to, change. They learn from others. Thus a circle emerges of learning and understanding. 'Most organizations do quite well in single-loop learning but have great difficulties in double-loop learning,' conclude Argyris and Schon.

In addition, Argyris and Schon propose a final form of learning which offers even greater challenges. This is 'deutero-learning' which they describe as 'inquiring into the learning system by which an organization detects and corrects its errors'. It is here, in the examination of learning systems, where the roots of contemporary concepts of the learning organization can most easily be found.

Since *Organizational Learning*, Argyris has continued to chart the deficiencies of learning processes and the natural temptation for organizations and individuals to limit themselves to single-loop learning rather than its more demanding alternatives. The need to understand learning better in all its dimensions is now imperative, says Argyris (1991): 'Any company that aspires to succeed in the tougher business environment of the 1990s must first resolve a basic dilemma: success in the marketplace increasingly depends on learning, yet most people don't know how to learn. What's more, those members of the organization that many assume to be the best at learning are, in fact, not very good at it.' The challenge – and mystery – of learning remains profound.

3

CHESTER BARNARD

The Functions of the Executive

1938

Hamel on Barnard

"Each new generation suffers from the conceit that the problems it faces are unique. Anyone who re-reads Barnard's landmark tome, published nearly 60 years ago, will quickly realize that the context of management changes faster than the 'functions of the executive'. As we worship the cult of the new, it is sometimes helpful to hark back to the wisdom of the old."

Chester Barnard (1886–1961)

Chester Barnard was a rarity: a management theorist who was also a successful practitioner. After a spell at Harvard, Barnard joined American Telephone and Telegraph to begin work as a statistician. He spent his entire working life with the company, eventually becoming President of New Jersey Bell in 1927.

Barnard remained with the company until his retirement in 1952. His interests were varied. During World War Two he worked as special assistant to the Secretary of the Treasury and co-wrote a report which formed the basis of US atomic energy policy.

Barnard's work has largely been ignored save for occasional bursts of interest when a contemporary guru uncovers a copy of *The Functions of the Executive*.

C hester Barnard's *The Functions of the Executive* is a book of his lectures on the subject of management. The language is dated, the approach ornate, but comprehensive. 'It is doubtful if any other book since Taylor's *Scientific Management* has had a deeper influence on the thinking of serious business leaders about the nature of their work,' observed Barnard's contemporary, Lyndall Urwick.

Indeed, there are many messages in *The Functions of the Executive* which resonate with contemporary management thinking. Barnard, for example, highlights the need for communication. He argues that everyone needs to know what and where the communications channels are so that each person can be tied into the organization's objectives. He also advocates lines of communication which are short and direct. 'The essential functions are, first, to provide the system of communications; second, to promote the securing of essential efforts; and, third, to formulate and define purpose,' he writes.

To Barnard the chief executive is not a dictatorial figure geared to simple short-term achievements. Part of his responsibility must be to nurture the values and goals of the organization. Barnard argues that values and goals need to be translated into action rather than meaningless motivational phraseology – 'strictly speaking, purpose is defined more nearly by the aggregate of action taken than by any formulation in words.'

This struck a chord with Peters and Waterman who, in *In Search of Excellence*, said that *The Functions of the Executive* 'probably deserves to be called a complete management theory'. The broad scope of Barnard's work was also identified by Harvard's Kenneth Andrews (Andrews, 1968) in his introduction to an anniversary edition of the book: 'Barnard's aim is ambitious. As he tells us in his own preface, his purpose is first to provide a comprehensive theory of cooperative behavior in formal organizations. Cooperation originates in the need of an individual to accomplish purposes to which he is by himself biologically unequal.'

There is a hint of Taylor's *Scientific Management* in such observations, but Barnard also proposes a moral dimension to the world of work (one which Taylor certainly did not recognize). 'The distinguishing mark of the executive responsibility is that it requires not merely conformance to a complex code of morals but also the creation of moral codes for others,' writes Barnard.

Barnard takes what would today be called a holistic approach arguing that 'in a community all acts of individuals and of organizations are directly or indirectly interconnected and interdependent'. Even so, for all his contemporary sounding ideas, Barnard was a man of his times – advocating corporate domination of the individual and regarding loyalty to the organization as paramount.

4

CHRISTOPHER BARTLETT & SUMANTRA GHOSHAL

Managing Across Borders

1989

Hamel on Bartlett & Ghoshal

"Many of the companies that expanded internationally in the early decades of the twentieth century, woke up in the 1970s and 1980s and found themselves seriously behind the integration curve as trade barriers crumbled and customer needs converged. Bartlett and Ghoshal chronicle the quest of these companies to become 'transnationals'. In urging companies to develop dense networks of horizontal communication, transfer learning laterally, and embed a sense of reciprocity among far-flung organizational units, they give a tangible meaning to the concept of a borderless company.**"**

CHRISTOPHER BARTLETT & SUMANTRA GHOSHAL

Australian-born, **Christopher Bartlett** was born in 1943. He is Professor of Business Administration at Harvard Business School.

Sumantra Ghoshal (born 1948) is Robert P. Bauman Professor of Strategic Leadership at London Business School. He joined London Business School in 1994 and was formerly Professor of Business Policy at INSEAD and a visiting professor at MIT's Sloan School. He is also the author of *Transnational Management: Text, Cases and Readings* (1990); *Organization Theory and the Multinational Corporation* (with Eleanor Westney, 1993) and *The Strategy Process: European Perspective* (with Henry Mintzberg and J.B. Quinn, 1995).

C hristopher Bartlett and Sumantra Ghoshal have emerged as perhaps the most complete commentators on the global business stage. Their work is carefully argued and contains a strong historical perspective. They poignantly and persuasively describe the new world order of the late 1990s, putting it in the context of the post-war business environment as a whole. Bartlett and Ghoshal point out that the 1990s are characterized by slow growth and overcapacity in many crucial industries – they calculate that there is 40 percent overcapacity in automobiles, 100 percent in bulk chemicals, 50 percent in steel, and 140 percent in computers.

In such an environment, mapped out in *Managing Across Borders*, historical solutions no are no longer applicable. For example, Bartlett and Ghoshal point to the difficulties in managing growth through acquisitions and the dangerously high level of diversity in businesses which have acquired companies indiscriminately in the quest for growth. Also obsolete in the 1990s is the assumption of independence among different businesses, technologies and geographic markets which is central to the design of most divisionalized corporations. Such independence, say Bartlett and Ghoshal, actively works against the prime need: integration and the creation of 'a coherent system for value delivery'.

Bartlett and Ghoshal observe – and celebrate – the demise of the multi-divisional form championed by Alfred P. Sloan among others. They recognize, however, that 'the multi-divisional organization was perhaps the single most important administrative innovation that helped companies grow in size and diversity far beyond the limits of the functional organization it replaced'.

The multi-divisional form, they say, is handicapped by having 'no process through which institutionalized wisdoms can be challenged, existing knowledge bases can be overturned, and the sources of the data can be reconfigured. In the absence of this challenge, these companies gradually become immobilized by conventional wisdoms that have ossified as sacred cows, and become constrained by outmoded knowledge and expertise that are out of touch with their rapidly changing realities'.

They describe the multidivisional approach as a 'doctrine – it is more than a mere specification of the organization structure: it also describes the roles and responsibilities of corporate, divisional and business unit level managers; relative status and norms of behavior of staff and line functionaries; machinisms and processes for allocation of resources; and, in general, "the rules of the game" inside the company. Over the last ten years, a variety of changes in market, technological and competitive contexts has rendered this doctrine obsolete and the problems large corporations are facing stem, at least in part, from sticking to this past success formula well beyond the limit of its usefulness'.

Bartlett and Ghoshal, unlike others, suggest that new, revitalizing, organizational forms can – and are – emerging. Crucial to this is the recognition that multinational corporations from different regions of the world have their own management heritages, each with a distinctive source of competitive advantage.

The first multinational form identified by Bartlett and Ghoshal is the **multinational** or multidomestic firm. Its strength lies in a high degree of local responsiveness. It is a decentralized federation of local firms (such as Unilever or Philips) linked together by a web of personal controls (expatriates from the home country firm who occupy key positions abroad).

The **global** firm is typified by US corporations such as Ford earlier this century and Japanese enterprises such as Matsushita. Its strengths are scale efficiencies and cost advantages. Global scale facilities, often centralized in the home country, produce standardized products, while overseas operations are considered as delivery pipelines to tap into global market opportunities. There is tight control of strategic decisions, resources and information by the global hub.

The **international** firm is the third type. Its competitive strength is its ability to transfer knowledge and expertise to overseas environments that are less advanced. It is a coordinated federation of local firms, controlled by sophisticated management systems and corporate staffs. The attitude of the parent company tends to be parochial, fostered by the superior knowhow at the center. This is the heritage of many American and some European firms. Bartlett and Ghoshal argue that global competition is forcing many of these firms to shift to a fourth model, which they call the **transnational**. This firm has to combine local responsiveness with global efficiency and the ability to transfer knowhow – better, cheaper, and faster.

The transnational firm is a network of specialized or differentiated units, with attention paid to managing integrative linkages between local firms as well as with the center. The subsidiary becomes a distinctive asset rather than simply an arm of the parent company. Manufacturing and technology development are located wherever it makes sense, but there is an explicit focus on leveraging local knowhow in order to exploit worldwide opportunities.

With these differing organizational forms available, Bartlett and Ghoshal argue that companies should do whatever makes sense for their business rather than following the organizational models of the past with the two extremes of centralization and decentralization.

Bartlett and Ghoshal also believe that companies possess 'organizational psychology' – 'a set of explicit or implicit shared values and beliefs – that can be developed and managed just as effectively as the organizational anatomy and physiology. For companies operating in an international environment, this is a particularly important organizational attribute'. In transnational organizations Bartlett and Ghoshal say that there are three techniques crucial to forming an organization's psychology. First, there must be 'clear, shared understanding of the company's mission and objectives'. Second, the actions and behavior of senior managers are vital as examples and statements of commitment. Third, corporate personnel policies must be geared up to 'develop a multi-dimensional and flexible organization process'.

Since *Managing Across Borders*, Bartlett and Ghoshal have developed their concepts still further and now describe an emerging organizational model: the entrepreneurial corporation. This is built on three core processes. The **entrepreneurial process** which drives the opportunity-seeking, externally focused ability of the organization to create new businesses. The **integration process** allows it to link and leverage its dispersed resources and competencies to build a successful company. The **renewal process** maintains its capacity to challenge its own beliefs and practices and to continuously revitalize itself so as to develop an enduring institution.

Each process, say Bartlett and Ghoshal, demands certain organizational infrastructures and mechanisms. Managing all three simultaneously requires a management mindset that is fundamentally different from the one that has been shaped so firmly over the last five decades by the doctrine of the multi-divisional enterprise.

5

MEREDITH BELBIN

Management Teams: Why they succeed or fail

1984

Hamel on Belbin

"High-performing companies increasingly believe that teams, rather than business units or individuals, are the basic building blocks of a successful organization. Belbin deserves much credit for helping us understand the basic building blocks of successful teams."

Meredith Belbin

The British academic Meredith Belbin is the doyen of the theory of teamworking. He read Classics and Psychology at Cambridge University before becoming a researcher at the Cranfield College of Aeronautics. He worked in Paris for the Organization for Economic Cooperation and Development and in a number of manufacturing companies.

Belbin's other books include *Team Roles at Work* (1993) and *The Coming Shape of Organization* (1996).

n his foreword to *Management Teams* Antony Jay writes: 'Corporations have been preoccupied with the qualifications, experience and achievement of individuals; they have applied themselves to the selection, development, training, motivation, and promotion of individuals; they have discussed and debated the strengths and weaknesses of individuals; and yet all of us know in our hearts that the ideal individual for a given job cannot be found. He cannot be found because he cannot exist.' Jay goes on to conclude that 'it is not the individual but the team that is the instrument of sustained and enduring success in management'.

In 1967 the UK's Henley Management College introduced a computer-based business game onto one of its courses. In this game, known as the Executive Management Exercise, 'company' teams of members competed to achieve the best score, according to the criteria laid down in the exercise. Henley arranged to collaborate with Meredith Belbin, then with the Industrial Training Research Unit at University College, London.

Belbin was interested in group performance and how it might be influenced by the kinds of people making up a group. Members engaging in the exercise were asked, voluntarily and confidentially, to undertake a personality and critical-thinking test. From his observations, based on the test results, Belbin discovered that certain combinations of personality types performed more successfully than others. Belbin began to be able to predict the winner of the game and realized that given adequate knowledge of the personal characteristics and abilities of team members through psychometric testing, he could forecast the likely success or failure of particular teams. As a result, unsuccessful teams can be improved by analyzing their team design shortcomings and making appropriate changes.

Belbin's first practical application of this work involved a questionnaire which managers filled out for themselves. The questionnaire was then analyzed to show the function roles the managers thought they performed in a team. This had one drawback: what *you* think you do is not of much value if the people with whom you work think differently. Belbin refined his methods and worked with others to design a computer program to do the job. (His work is now available on CD-ROM.)

From his first-hand observation at Henley's unique 'laboratory', Belbin identified nine archetypal functions which go to make up an ideal team. These are:

- **plant** – creative, imaginative, unorthodox; solves difficult problems. Allowable weakness: bad at dealing with ordinary people.
- **coordinator** – mature, confident, trusting; a good chairman; clarifies goals, promotes decision making. Not necessarily the cleverest.
- **shaper** – dynamic, outgoing, highly strung; challenges, pressurizes, finds ways round obstacles. Prone to bursts of temper.
- **teamworker** – social, mild, perceptive, accommodating; listens, builds, averts friction. Indecisive in crunch situations.
- **completer** – painstaking, conscientious, anxious; searches out errors; delivers on time. May worry unduly; reluctant to delegate.
- **implementer** – disciplined, reliable, conservative, efficient; turns ideas into actions. Somewhat inflexible.
- **resource investigator** – extrovert, enthusiastic, communicative; explores opportunities. Loses interest after initial enthusiasm.
- **specialist** – single-minded, self-starting, dedicated; brings knowledge or skills in rare supply. Contributes only on narrow front.
- **monitor evaluator** – sober, strategic, discerning. Sees all options, makes judgments. Lacks drive and ability to inspire others.

These categories have proved robust and are still used in a variety of organizations. The explosion of interest in team-working during the last decade has prompted greater interest in Belbin's work. He has since continued to refine and expand his theories in a series of books.

6

WARREN BENNIS & BURT NANUS

Leaders: The Strategies for Taking Charge

1985

Hamel on Bennis & Nanus

"Here we find the antithesis of a technocratic view of management. This truly is a book about leaders, not about managers. And while Bennis and Nanus succeeded in isolating the deep attributes of leadership, I remain unconvinced that leadership can be taught. Nevertheless, I am absolutely convinced that we must all aspire to be leaders. A heartfelt thanks to Warren and Burt for helping us raise our sights."

Warren Bennis & Burt Nanus

Warren Bennis' lengthy career has involved him in education, writing, consulting and administration. Born in 1925, he was the youngest infantry officer in the European theater of operations during World War Two; an early student of group dynamics in the 1950s; a futurologist in the 1960s and the world's premier leadership theorist in the 1970s and 1980s.

Bennis studied under Douglas McGregor at Antioch College and later became an academic administrator – he was Provost at SUNY, Buffalo (1967–71); and President of the University of Cincinnati between 1971 and 1978. He is now Distinguished Professor of Business Administration at the University of Southern California and is founder and chairman of the school's Leadership Institute. Psychologist Abraham Maslow described Bennis as 'one of the Olympian minds of our time'. In his book *Future Shock*, Alvin Toffler claimed: 'If it was Max Weber who first defined bureaucracy, and predicted its triumph, Warren Bennis may go down as the man who first convincingly predicted its demise and sketched the outlines of the organizations that are springing up to replace it.'

Burt Nanus was Bennis' co-author and founder and director of the Center of Futures Research at the University of Southern California.

arren Bennis and Burt Nanus' *Leaders: The Strategies for Taking Charge* is a thoroughly populist book following the conventional formula of seeking out lessons on how to become successful from successful people. It is based on Bennis' research with 90 of America's leaders. While the book's formula is hackneyed, it is given an extra dimension by the eclectic selection of leaders. They include Neil Armstrong; the coach of the LA Rams; orchestral conductors; and businessmen such as Ray Kroc of McDonald's. 'They were right-brained and left-brained, tall and short, fat and thin, articulate and inarticulate, assertive and retiring, dressed for success and dressed for failure, participative and autocratic,' says Bennis.[1] The link between them is that they have all shown 'mastery over present confusion'. The message is that leadership is all-encompassing and open to all.

From the 90 leaders, four common abilities are identified: management of attention; of meaning; of trust; and of self.

Management of attention is, says Bennis, a question of vision. Indeed, he uses a definition of leadership as: 'The capacity to create a compelling vision and translate it into action and sustain it.' Successful leaders have a vision that other people believe in and treat as their own.

Having a vision is one thing, converting it into successful action is another. The second skill shared by Bennis' selection of leaders is management of meaning – communications. A vision is of limited practical use if it is encased in 400 pages of wordy text or mumbled from behind a paper-packed desk. Bennis believes effective communication relies on use of analogy, metaphor and vivid illustration as well as emotion, trust, optimism and hope.

The third aspect of leadership identified by Bennis is trust which he describes as 'the emotional glue that binds followers and leaders together'. Leaders have to be seen to be consistent.

The final common bond between the 90 leaders studied by Bennis is 'deployment of self'. The leaders do not glibly present charisma or time management as the essence of their success. Instead, the emphasis is on persistence and self-knowledge, taking risks, commitment and challenge but, above all, learning. 'The learning person looks forward to failure or mistakes,' says Bennis. 'The worst problem in leadership is basically early success. There's no opportunity to learn from adversity and problems.'

The leaders have a positive self-regard, what Bennis labels 'emotional wisdom'. This is characterized by an ability to accept people as they are; a capacity to approach things only in terms of the present; an ability to treat everyone, even close contacts, with courteous attention; an ability to trust others even when this seems risky; and an ability to do without constant approval and recognition.

Leadership, Bennis believes, can be learnt. He is an optimist and this lies at the heart of his work, and *Leaders* in particular: 'Every person has to make a genuine contribution in their lives. The institution of work is one of the main vehicles to achieving this. I'm more and more convinced that individual leaders can create a human community that will, in the long run, lead to the best organizations.'[2]

If this is to be achieved, five myths of leadership need to be overcome. First, it needs to be understood that leadership is not a rare skill. Second, that leaders are made rather than born. Third, leaders are mostly ordinary people – or apparently ordinary – rather than charismatic. Fourth, leadership is not solely the preserve of those at the top of the organization – it is relevant at all levels. And, finally, leadership is not about control, direction and manipulation. Instead, leaders align the energies of others behind an attractive goal.

Leaders was a bestseller and cemented Warren Bennis' reputation as one of the world's premier leadership theorists. Its importance lies not in the common characteristics of leaders identified in the book, but in its exploding of the myth of the leader as a hero. In the hands of Bennis and Nanus, leadership is fundamentally humane, human and achievable.

Bennis has continued to explore the subject in his subsequent books which include *On Becoming a Leader* (1989); *Why Leaders Can't Lead* (1989); and *Organizing Genius: The Secrets of Creative Collaboration* (1997).

Notes
1 Quoted in Crainer, Stuart, 'Doing the right thing', *The Director*, October 1988.
2 Ibid.

7

JAMES MacGREGOR BURNS

Leadership

1978

Hamel on Burns

"There is no theme in management literature which is more enduring than leadership. Among the many contributions which Burns makes to our understanding of leadership, two seem central: leadership must have a moral foundation; and the responsibility for leadership must be widely distributed. Self-interested autocrats, whether political or corporate, ignore these truths at their peril."

James MacGregor Burns

James MacGregor Burns is a political scientist. Not simply a theorist, he has stood, unsuccessfully, for Congress as a Democrat and worked in John F. Kennedy's presidential campaign.

His books include *Congress on Trial* (1949); *Government by the People* (with Jack Peltason, 1950); *Roosevelt: The Lion and the Fox* (1956); *John Kennedy: A Political Profile* (1960); *The Deadlock of Democracy* (1963); *Presidential Government: The Crucible of Leadership* (1965); *Roosevelt: The Soldier of Freedom* (1970); *Uncommon Sense* (1972) and *Edward Kennedy and the Camelot Legacy* (1976).

'T'he crisis of leadership today is the mediocrity or irresponsibility of so many of the men and women in power, but leadership rarely rises to the full need for it. The fundamental crisis underlying mediocrity is intellectual. If we know all too much about our leaders, we know far too little about leadership,' observes James MacGregor Burns in the prologue to *Leadership*.

There are literally hundreds of definitions of leadership. Burns suggests that, as a result, 'leadership as a concept has dissolved into small and discrete meanings. A superabundance of facts about leaders far outruns theories of leadership.' Undaunted, in *Leadership*, Burns provides yet another – but one which has proved more enduring: 'Leadership over human beings is exercised when persons with certain motives and purposes mobilize, in competition or conflict with others, institutional, political, psychological and other resources so as to arouse, engage and satisfy the motives of followers.'

To Burns, leadership is not the preserve of the few or the tyranny of the masses. 'The leadership approach tends often unconsciously to be elitist; it projects heroic figures against the shadowy background of drab, powerless masses,' he writes. 'The followership approach tends to be populistic or anti-elitist in ideology; it perceives the masses, even in democratic societies, as linked with small, overlapping circles of conservative politicians, military officers, hierocrats, and businessmen. I describe leadership here as no mere game among elitists and no mere populist response but as a structure of action that engages persons, to varying degrees, throughout the levels and among the interstices of society. Only the inert, the alienated, and the powerless are unengaged.' To Burns, leadership is intrinsically linked to morality and 'moral leadership emerges from, and always returns to, the fundamental wants and needs, aspirations, and values of the followers'.

Aside from his thoughtful definition, in *Leadership*, Burns identifies two vital strands of leadership – transformational and transactional leadership.

Transformational leadership 'occurs when one or more persons engage with others in such a way that leaders and followers raise one another to higher levels of motivation and morality. Their purposes, which might have started out separate but related ... become fused. Power bases are linked not as counterweights but as mutual support for common purpose,' writes Burns. 'Various names are used for such leadership: elevating, mobilizing, inspiring, exalting, uplifting, exhorting, evangelizing. The relationship can be moralistic, of course. But transforming leadership ultimately becomes moral in that it raises the level of human conduct and ethical aspiration of both the leader and the led, and thus has a transforming effect on both ... Transforming leadership is dynamic leadership in the sense that the leaders throw themselves into a relationship with followers who will feel "elevated" by it and often become more active themselves, thereby creating new cadres of leaders.'

Transformational leadership is concerned with engaging the hearts and minds of others. It works to help all parties achieve greater motivation, satisfaction and a greater sense of achievement. It is driven by trust and concern and facilitation rather than direct control. The skills required are concerned with establishing a long-term vision, empowering people to control themselves, coaching and developing others and challenging the culture to change. In transformational leadership, the power of the leader comes from creating understanding and trust.

Alternatively, transactional leadership is built on repricocity, the idea that the relationship between leaders and their followers develops from the exchange of some reward, such as performance ratings, pay, recognition and praise. In involves leaders clarifying goals and objectives, communicating to organize tasks and activities with the cooperation of their employees to ensure that wider organizational goals are met.

Such a relationship depends on hierarchy and the ability to work through the mode of exchange. It requires leadership skills, such as the ability to obtain results, to control through structures and processes, to solve problems, to plan and organize and work within the structures and boundaries of the organization.

In their apparent mutual exclusiveness, transformational and transactional leadership are akin to Douglas McGregor's Theories X and Y. The secret of effective leadership appears to lie in combining the two elements so that targets, results and procedures are developed and shared.

Burns' book provides an important link between leadership in the political and business worlds. For all the books on leadership, these two fields of activity have usually been regarded as mutually exclusive. His examination of transformational and transactional leadership also stimulated further debate on leadership at a time when it was somewhat neglected. In the 1980s it returned to prominence in management literature as a subject worthy of study.

8

DALE CARNEGIE

How to Win Friends and Influence People

1937

Hamel on Carnegie

"I recently attended a conference with the title 'Implementing strategy through people'. I asked the sponsor whether there was an alternative – perhaps one could implement strategy through dogs. When the focus is on technology, structure and process it is easy to lose sight of the deeply personal nature of management. Though Dale Carnegie's advice sometimes borders on the manipulative, it is a warm and fuzzy, eager salesman kind of manipulation. What a contrast to the hard-edged, got-you-by-your-paycheck manipulation familiar to thousands of anxiety-ridden survivors of corporate restructuring.**"**

Dale Carnegie

Born on a Missouri farm, **Dale Carnegie** began his working life selling bacon, soap and lard for Armour & Company in south Omaha. He turned his sales territory into the company's national leader, but then went to New York to study at the American Academy of Dramatic Arts – he toured the country as Dr. Harley in *Polly of the Circus*. Realizing the limits of his acting potential, Carnegie returned to salesmanship – selling Packard automobiles. It was then that Carnegie persuaded the YMCA schools in New York to allow him to conduct courses in public speaking.

Carnegie's talks became highly successful. He wrote *Public Speaking and Influencing Men in Business* and a variety of other variations on his theme – *How to Stop Worrying and Start Living*, *How to Enjoy Your Life and Your Job*, *How to Develop Self-Confidence and Influence People by Public Speaking*. He is best known, however, for *How to Win Friends and Influence People* which has sold over 15 million copies (its first edition had a print run of a mere 5,000). Dale Carnegie died in 1955.

D ale Carnegie's *How to Win Friends and Influence People* is the original self-improvement book. 'If by the time you have finished reading the first three chapters of this book you aren't then a little better equipped to meet life's situations, then I shall consider this book to be a total failure,' Carnegie writes in its opening. It was written by Carnegie as a textbook for his courses in 'Effective speaking and human relations'. Carnegie's aim was to write 'a practical, working handbook on human relations'.

To do so, Carnegie eagerly explains that no stone was left unturned. He read extensively and hired a researcher to spend 18 months reading the books he had missed – 'I recall that we read over one hundred biographies of Theodore Roosevelt alone'. Carnegie then interviewed some famous names – from Clark Gable to Marconi, Franklin D. Roosevelt to Mary Pickford.

Carnegie was a salesman *extraordinaire*. Names are dropped, promises made. Up-beat and laden with sentiment, *How to Win Friends and Influence People* is a simple selling document – 'The rules we have set down here are not mere theories or guesswork. They work like magic. Incredible as it sounds, I have seen the application of these principles literally revolutionize the lives of many people.'

The result is a number of principles from which friends and influence should, Carnegie anticipates, surely emerge. First, there are the 'fundamental techniques in handling people' – 'don't criticize, condemn or complain; give honest and sincere appreciation; and arouse in the other person an eager want'. Then Carnegie presents six ways to make people like you – 'become genuinely interested in other people; smile; remember that a person's name is to that person the sweetest and most important sound in any language; be a good listener. Encourage others to talk about themselves; talk in terms of the other person's interests; make the other person feel important – and do it sincerely.'

Carnegie's advice comes adorned with a host of anecdotes from the famous to the not so famous – characters such as George Dyke of North Warren, Pennsylvania, who 'was forced to retire from his service station business after thirty years when a new highway was constructed over the site of the station'. Undeterred, Dyke became a traveling fiddler in demand throughout the country.

It is easy to be critical and cynical of much of what is written in *How to Win Friends and Influence People*. In one interview, Peter Drucker dismissed the self-help genre as based on the hope that 'you can make a million and still go to heaven'. However, there is a perennial demand – and, presumably, a need – for such books. Indeed, there are echoes of Carnegie in many books published even now. Peters and Waterman's celebration of customer service owes something to Carnegie's advice on 'the big secret of dealing with people' and books by the like of Mark McCormack are often simply contemporary versions of the truisms espoused by Carnegie over half a century earlier.

Carnegie's message remains relevant: people matter and, in the world of business, how you manage and relate to people is the key to success.

9

JAMES CHAMPY & MICHAEL HAMMER

Reengineering the Corporation

1993

Hamel on Champy & Hammer

"Scientific management, industrial engineering, business process improvement, and now, new and improved, reengineering. The idea might be old, but the language was new and the time was right. A brutally tough competitive environment and the explosion of information technology compelled companies to take a fresh look at inefficient and sclerotic processes. Too bad reengineering usually exacted the same human toll as restructuring – fewer, more cynical employees. If Champy and Hammer want to make a killing, the next book will be titled *Reenergizing!*"

James Champy &
Michael Hammer

James Champy is co-founder of the consultancy company CSC Index. CSC has become one of the largest consultancy companies in the world with revenues in excess of $500 million and over 2,000 consultants worldwide. Champy is also the author of *Reengineering Management: The Mandate for New Leadership* (1995).

Michael Hammer (born 1948) is a former computer science professor at MIT and President of Hammer and Company, a management education and consulting firm. He is widely credited with being the founding father of reengineering. Its roots lie in the research carried out by MIT from 1984 to 1989 on 'Management in the 1990s'. Hammer's sequel was *The Reengineering Revolution* (with Steven Stanton, 1995).

R eengineering was unquestionably the business idea of the first half of the 1990s. James Champy and Michael Hammer's *Reengineering the Corporation* was the manifesto for a promised revolution, one that has – except in a few instances – largely failed to materialize. The claims made for reengineering and for Champy and Hammer's book, are large. 'When people ask me what I do for a living, I tell them that what I really do is I'm reversing the Industrial Revolution,' proclaims Hammer. Indeed, the opening of the book positions it as the ready replacement for Adam Smith's *The Wealth of Nations*. It has now sold over two million copies.

Cutting away the hype and hyperbole, the basic idea behind reengineering is that organizations need to identify their key processes and make them as lean and efficient as possible. Peripheral processes (and, therefore, peripheral people) need to be discarded. Champy and Hammer define reengineering as 'the fundamental rethinking and radical redesign of business processes to achieve dramatic improvements in critical measures of performance such as cost, quality, service and speed'.

To Champy and Hammer, reengineering is more than dealing with mere processes. They eschew the popular phrase 'business process reengineering', regarding it as too limiting. In their view the scope and scale of reengineering goes far beyond simply altering and refining processes. True reengineering is all-embracing.

In *Reengineering the Corporation*, Champy and Hammer advocate that companies equip themselves with a blank piece of paper and map out their processes. 'It is time to stop paving the cow paths. Instead of imbedding outdated processes in silicon and software, we should obliterate them and start over,' pronounced Hammer with characteristic fervor and idiosyncratic imagery in his *Harvard Business Review* article (Hammer, 1990) which set the reengineering bandwagon rolling. Having come up with a neatly engineered map of how their business should operate, companies can then attempt to translate the paper theory into concrete reality.

The concept is simple. (Indeed, critics of reengineering regard it as a contemporary version of Taylor's *The Principles of Scientific Management* with its belief in measurement and optimal ways of completing particular tasks.) Making it happen has proved immensely more difficult. The first problem is that the blank piece of paper ignores the years, often decades, of cultural evolution which have led to an organization doing something in a certain way. Such preconceptions are not easily discarded. Indeed, discarding them may well amount to corporate suicide.

Champy and Hammer say that reengineering is concerned with 'rejecting conventional wisdom and received assumptions of the past ... it is about reversing the industrial revolution ... tradition counts for nothing. Reengineering is a new beginning'. In *Leaning into the Future* (Binney and Williams, 1995), British academics Colin Williams and George Binney are dismissive of such talk: 'The last time someone used language like this was Chairman Mao in the Cultural Revolution. Under the motto "Destroy to build", he too insisted on sweeping away the past. Instead of such wanton destruction, successful organizations do not deny or attempt to destroy the inheritance of the past. They seek to build on it. They try to understand in depth why they have been successful and they try to do more of it. They are respectful of the learning accumulated from experience and recognize that much of this learning is not made explicit at the top of the organization.'

Henry Mintzberg (1996) has also expressed his concern about reengineering. 'There is no reengineering in the idea of reengineering,' he says. 'Just reification, just the same old notion that the new system will do the job. But because of the hype that goes with any new management fad, everyone has to run around reengineering everything. We are supposed to get superinnovation on demand just because it is deemed necessary by a manager in some distant office who has read a book. Why don't we just stop reengineering and delayering and restructuring and decentralizing and instead start thinking?'

The second problem is that reengineering has become a synonym for redundancy. For this Champy and Hammer cannot be entirely blamed. Often, companies which claim to be reengineering are simply engaging in cost-cutting under the convenient guise of the fashionable theory. Downsizing appears more publicly palatable if it is presented as implementing a leading edge concept. In 1994, research covering 624 companies, published in *The State of Reengineering*, CSC Index found that on average 336 jobs were lost per reengineering project in the US and 760 in Europe.

The third obstacle which has emerged is that corporations are not natural or even willing revolutionaries. Instead of casting the reengineering net widely they tend to reengineer the most readily accessible process and then leave it at that. Related to this, and the subject of Champy's sequel, *Reengineering Management*, reengineering usually fails to impinge on management. Managers are all too willing to impose the rigors of a process-based view of the business on others, but often unwilling to inflict it upon themselves.

Champy (1994) has now concluded that it is 'time to reengineer the manager': 'Senior managers have been reengineering business processes with a passion, tearing down corporate structures that no longer can support the organization. Yet the practice of management has largely escaped demolition. If their jobs and styles are left largely intact, managers will eventually undermine the very structure of their rebuilt enterprises.' Champy suggests reengineering management should tackle three key areas: managerial roles, managerial styles and managerial systems.

It is the human side of reengineering which has proved the greatest stumbling block. 'Most reengineering efforts will fail or fall short of the mark because of the absence of trust –

meaning respect for the individual, his or her goodwill, intelligence and native, but long shackled, curiosity,' observed Tom Peters (July 1993).

In his review of the book in the *Financial Times*, Christopher Lorenz (1993) noted: 'They [Champy and Hammer] are ... inconsistent about whether they think behavioral and cultural change ... are an automatic result of the reengineering of business processes or whether such soft change needs to be launched in parallel or even beforehand. Controversially much of the book suggests that soft follows hard automatically.'

Champy and Hammer would counter that true reengineering is actually built on trust, respect and people. By cutting away peripheral activities companies provide an environment which places a premium on the skills and potential of those it employs. This, as yet, has not been supported by corporate experience – though James Champy believes the best is yet to come. 'There are at least another 10 years of genuine reengineering to run,' he predicts.

10

ALFRED CHANDLER

Strategy and Structure

1962

Hamel on Chandler

"Those who dispute Chandler's thesis that structure follows strategy miss the point. Of course strategy and structure are inextricably intertwined. Chandler's point was that new challenges give rise to new structures. The challenges of size and complexity, coupled with advances in communications and techniques of management control produced divisionalization and decentralization. These same forces, several generations on, are now driving us towards new structural solutions – the 'federated organization', the multi-company coalition, and the virtual company. Few historians are prescient. Chandler was.**"**

Alfred Chandler

Alfred Chandler (born 1918) is a Pulitzer Prize-winning business historian. After graduating from Harvard, he served in the US Navy before becoming, somewhat unusually, a historian at MIT in 1950. Later he became Professor of History at Johns Hopkins University. He has been Straus Professor of Business History at Harvard since 1971. His hugely detailed research into US companies between 1850 and 1920 has formed the cornerstone of much of his work.

lfred Chandler's *Strategy and Structure* is a theoretical masterpiece which has had profound influence on both practitioners and thinkers. Its sub-title is 'Chapters in the history of the American industrial enterprise', but its impact went far beyond that of a brilliantly researched historical text.

From his research into major US corporations between 1850 and 1920, Chandler argues that a firm's structure is dictated by its chosen strategy – 'Unless structure follows strategy, inefficiency results'. First, a company should establish a strategy and then seek to create the structure appropriate to achieving it. Chandler defines strategy as 'the determination of the long-term goals and objectives of an enterprise, and the adoption of courses of action and the allocation of resources necessary for carrying out these goals'.

Chandler observes that organizational structures in companies such as DuPont, Sears Roebuck, General Motors and Standard Oil were driven by the changing demands and pressures of the marketplace. He traces the market-driven proliferation of product lines in DuPont and General Motors and concludes that this proliferation led to a shift from a functional, monolithic organizational form to a more loosely-coupled divisional structure. (Interestingly, Chandler's family has historical connections with DuPont – and DuPont is, in fact, Chandler's middle name. At the time DuPont also controlled General Motors.)

Until recent times, Chandler's conclusion that structure follows strategy has largely been accepted as a fact of corporate life. Now, the debate has been rekindled. 'I think he got it exactly wrong,' says Tom Peters (1992) with typical forthrightness. 'For it is the structure of the organization that determines, over time, the choices that it makes about the markets it attacks.'

In *Managing on the Edge*, Richard Pascale (1990) observes: 'The underlying assumption is that organizations act in a rational, sequential manner. Yet most executives will readily agree that it is often the other way around. The way a company is organized, whether functional focused or driven by independent divisions, often plays a major role in shaping its strategy. Indeed, this accounts for the tendency of organizations to do what they best know how to do – regardless of deteriorating success against the competitive realities.'

While this debate rumbles on, Chandler's place in the canon of management literature remains secure. In particular, he was highly influential in the trend among large organizations for decentralization in the 1960s and 1970s. While in 1950 around 20 percent of *Fortune* 500 corporations were decentralized; this had increased to 80 percent by 1970. In *Strategy and Structure*, Chandler praises Alfred Sloan's decentralization of General Motors in the 1920s. He was later influential in the transformation of AT&T in the 1980s from what was in effect a production-based bureaucracy to a marketing organization.

In *Strategy and Structure* Chandler gives a historical context to the multi-divisional organization. Its chief advantage, he writes, is that 'it clearly removed the executives responsible for the destiny of the entire enterprise from the more routine operational responsibilities and so gave them the time, information and even psychological commitment for long-term planning and appraisal'.

Strategy and Structure also contributed to the 'professionalization of management'. Chandler traces the historical development of what he labels 'the managerial revolution' fueled by the rise of oil-based energy, the development of the steel, chemical and engineering industries and a dramatic rise in the scale of production and the size of companies. Increases in scale, Chandler observes, led to business owners having to recruit a new breed of professional manager.

Chandler believes that the roles of the salaried manager and technician are vital, and talks of the 'visible hand' of management coordinating the flow of product to customers more efficiently than Adam Smith's 'invisible hand' of the market (see Chandler's 1977 book, *The Visible Hand: The Managerial Revolution in American Business*). The logical progression from this is that organizations and their managements require a planned economy rather than a capitalist free-for-all dominated by the unpredictable whims of market forces. In the more sedate times in which *Strategy and Structure* was written, the lure of the visible hand proved highly persuasive.

11

W. EDWARDS DEMING

Out of the Crisis

1982

Hamel on Deming

"Of all the management gurus sandwiched between the covers of this book, there is only one who should be regarded as a hero by every consumer in the world – Dr. Deming. He may have taken the gospel of quality to the Japanese first, but thank God his message finally penetrated the smug complacency of American and European companies. I sat in a meeting where a worried American automobile executive inquired of Dr. Deming: 'When will we catch our Japanese competitors?' 'Hrmmph,' replied Dr. Deming, 'do you think they're standing still?' No senior executive ever sat through one of Dr. Deming's 'the rot starts at the top' harangues without coming away just a little bit more humble and contrite – a good start on the road to total quality."

W. Edwards Deming (1900–1993)

W. Edwards Deming has a unique place among management theorists. He had an impact on industrial history in a way others only dream of. Trained as an electrical engineer, Deming then received a Ph.D. in mathematical physics from Yale. Deming visited Japan after World War Two on the invitation of General MacArthur and played a key role in the rebuilding of Japanese industry. His impact was quickly recognized. He was awarded the Second Order of the Sacred Treasure and the Union of Japanese Scientists and Engineers instigated the annual Deming Prize in 1951.

During the 1950s, Deming and the other American standard bearer of quality, Joseph Juran, conducted seminars and courses throughout Japan. Between 1950 and 1970 the Japanese Union of Scientists and Engineers taught statistical methods to 14,700 engineers and hundreds of others.

Deming, and Japanese management, were eventually 'discovered' by the West in the 1980s and then only when NBC featured a program on the emergence of Japan as an industrial power ('If Japan can, why can't we?'). Suddenly, Western managers were seeking out every morsel of information they could find – in October 1991 *Business Week* published a bonus issue devoted exclusively to quality which sold out in a matter of days and ran to two special printings of tens of thousands of copies.

Though an old man, Deming traveled the world preaching his gospel to increasingly receptive audiences.

O ut of the Crisis was published near to the end of W. Edwards Deming's life and exists as a rather pallid representation of his lifetime's work. In Out of the Crisis, Deming distills quality down to a simple message. 'Profit in business comes from repeat customers, customers that boast about your product and service, and that bring friends with them,' he writes. While such beguiling home truths attracted a broader audience, they are only a shadow of Deming's all encompassing concept of what quality entails. 'The aim of this book is transformation of the style of American management,' says Deming.

For Deming, quality was more than statistical control though this was important. 'His work bridges the gap between science-based application and humanistic philosophy. Statistical quality control is as arid as it sounds. But results so spectacular as to be almost romantic flow from using these tools to improve processes in ways that minimize defects and eliminate the deadly trio of rejects, rework and recalls,' stated the British management commentator, Robert Heller (1994).

The quality gospel of Out of the Crisis revolves around a number of basic precepts. First, if consistent quality is to be achieved senior managers must take charge of quality. Second, implementation requires a 'cascade' with training beginning at the top of the organization before moving downwards through the hierarchy. Third, the use of statistical methods of quality control is necessary so that, finally, business plans can be expanded to include clear quality goals.

As summarized in his famous Fourteen Points, quality is a way of living, the meaning of industrial life and, in particular, the meaning of management – 'Management for quality' was Deming's constant refrain. Out of the Crisis presents a snappy version of Deming's Fourteen Points:

1 Create constancy of purpose for improvement of product and service.
2 Adopt the new philosophy.

3 Cease dependence on inspection to achieve quality.
4 End the practice of awarding business on the basis of price tag alone. Instead, minimize total cost by working with a single supplier.
5 Improve constantly and forever every process for planning, production and service.
6 Institute training on the job.
7 Adopt and institute leadership.
8 Drive out fear.
9 Break down barriers between staff areas.
10 Eliminate slogans, exhortations and targets for the workforce.
11 Eliminate numerical quotas for the workforce and numerical goals for management.
12 Remove barriers that rob people of pride of workmanship. Eliminate the annual rating or merit system.
13 Institute a vigorous program of education and self-improvement for everyone.
14 Put everybody in the company to work to accomplish the transformation.

The simplicity of the Fourteen Points disguises the immensity of the challenge, particularly that facing management. Quality, in Deming's eyes, is not the preserve of the few but the responsibility of all. In arguing this case Deming was anticipating the fashion for empowerment. 'People all over the world think that it is the factory worker that causes problems. He is not your problem,' observed Deming in a 1983 lecture at Utah State University. 'Ever since there has been anything such as industry, the factory worker has known that quality is what will protect his job. He knows that poor quality in the hands of the customer will lose the market and cost him his job. He knows it and lives with that fear very day. Yet he cannot do a good job. He is not allowed to do it because the management wants figures, more products, and never mind the quality.'

To Deming, management is 90 percent of the problem, a problem caused in part by the Western enthusiasm for annual performance appraisals – Deming points out that Japanese managers receive feedback every day of their working lives. 'The basic cause of sickness in American industry and resulting unemployment is failure of top management to manage. He that sells not can buy not,' writes Deming.

Indeed, the Japanese culture was uniquely receptive to Deming's message for a number of reasons. Its emphasis on group rather than individual achievement enables the Japanese to share ideas and responsibility, and promotes collective ownership in a way that the West often finds difficult to contemplate let alone understand.

Deming's evangelical fervor has played a part in his work being narrowly interpreted. Managers feel ill at ease with his exhortations and broad philosophical goals. Even so, Deming's ideas contain echoes of many current managerial preoccupations. In 1950, for example, Deming was anticipating reengineering with his call to arms: 'Don't just make it and try to sell it. But redesign it and then again bring the process under control ... with ever-increasing quality ... The consumer is the most important part of the production line.'

The longevity of Deming's particular interpretation of quality remains open to debate. The popularity of quality as a generic 'good thing' has tended to dilute the profundity of the changes in thinking and action propounded by Deming. Amid a host of short-lived initiatives and ungainly acronyms, managers and their organizations can appear to have firmly embraced Deming's theories. In practice this is not usually the case.

Even so, there is no questioning the enormous effect Deming's thinking has had – both in Japan and now in the West. The explosion of interest in quality in the 1980s, belated as it was, was principally stirred by Deming. 'Deming didn't invent "quality" ... but his sermons had a uniquely powerful effect because of this first pulpit and congregation:

Japan and Japanese managers. Had his fellow Americans responded with the same intense application, post-war industrial history would have differed enormously,' commented Robert Heller (1994) after Deming's death.

12

PETER F. DRUCKER

The Practice of Management

1954

Hamel on Drucker

"No other writer has contributed as much to the 'professionalization' of management as Peter Drucker. Drucker's commitment to the discipline of management grew out of his belief that industrial organizations would become, and would continue to be, the world's most important social organizations – more influential, more encompassing, and often more intrusive than either the church or the state. Professor Drucker bridges the theoretical and the practical, the analytical and the emotive, the private and the social more perfectly than any other management writer."

Peter F. Drucker

In South Korea there is a businessman who has changed his name to Drucker in the expectation that some of the brilliant insights of the Austrian-born thinker will be passed on to him. Such is the influence of **Peter Ferdinand Drucker** (born 1909), the major management and business thinker of the century. 'In a field packed with egomaniacs and snake-oil merchants, he remains a genuinely original thinker,' observes *The Economist*. Prolific, even in his eighties, Drucker's work is all-encompassing.

After working as a journalist in London, Drucker moved to America in 1937 and produced *Concept of the Corporation* in 1946. This groundbreaking work examined the intricate internal working of General Motors and revealed the auto-giant to be a labyrinthine social system rather than an economical machine.

His books have emerged regularly ever since. Along the way he has coined phrases such as *privatization* and *knowledge worker* and championed concepts such as *Management By Objectives*. Many of his innovations have become accepted facts of managerial life. He has celebrated huge organizations and anticipated their demise ('The *Fortune* 500 is over,' is one of his more recent aphorisms).

'In most areas of intellectual life nobody can quite agree who is top dog. In management theory, however, there is no dispute. Peter Drucker has produced groundbreaking work in every aspect of the field,' says *The Economist*.

Eschewing the academic glamour of the likes of Harvard, Drucker has been a professor at Claremont Graduate School in California since 1971. He also lectures in oriental art and has an abiding passion for Jane Austen though his two novels were less successful than his management books.

T *he Practice of Management* is a book of huge range. Encyclopedic in its scope and fulsome in its historical perspectives, for the humble practicing executive it is both daunting and inspiring. 'Management will remain a basic and dominant institution perhaps as long as Western civilization itself survives,' pronounces Peter Drucker. There is a dashing, and infectious, confidence to Drucker's tone. The book, he says in the preface, 'comes from many years of experience in working with managements'. At the time Drucker was in his early forties.

While *The Practice of Management* is important for its ideas, the tools and techniques of management, it is also important for the central role it argues management has in twentieth-century society. Drucker places management and managers at the epicenter of economic activity. 'Management is also a distinct and a leading group in industrial society,' he writes. 'Rarely, if ever, has a new basic institution, a new leading group, emerged as fast as has management since the turn of the century. Rarely in human history has a new institution proved indispensable so quickly.'

Bold and forthright as it is, *The Practice of Management* is also remarkable in its clarity. Drucker sets huge parameters for the art of management but reins them in through his masterly ability to return to first principles. Management may change the world, but its essence remains the same. In one of the most quoted and memorable paragraphs in management literature, Drucker gets to the heart of the meaning of business life. 'There is only one valid definition of business purpose: to create a customer. Markets are not created by God, nature or economic forces, but by businessmen. The want they satisfy may have been felt by the customer before he was offered the means of satisfying it. It may indeed, like the want of food in a famine, have dominated the customer's life and filled all his waking moments. But it was a theoretical want before; only when the action of businessmen makes it an effective demand is there a customer, a market.'

Drucker argues that, since the role of business was to create customers, its only two essential functions were marketing and innovation. In 1954 he wrote: 'Marketing is not a function, it is the whole business seen from the customer's point of view.' As markets have matured and become more competitive, especially during the 1990s, this 40-year-old concept has become increasingly widely accepted. (In his famous 1960 article, 'Marketing myopia', Harvard's Ted Levitt acknowledges his debt to Drucker's championing of marketing.)

Drucker also provides an evocatively simple insight into the nature and *raison d'être* of organizations: 'Organization is not an end in itself, but a means to an end of business performance and business results. Organization structure is an indispensable means, and the wrong structure will seriously impair business performance and may even destroy it... The first question in discussing organization structure must be: What is our business and what should it be? Organization structure must be designed so as to make possible the attainment of the objectives of the business for five, ten, fifteen years hence.'

In *The Practice of Management* and the equally enormous, *Management: Tasks, Responsibilities and Practices* in 1973, Drucker establishes five basics of the managerial role: to set objectives; to organize; motivate and communicate; to measure and to develop people. 'The function which distinguishes the manager above all others is his educational one,' he writes. 'The one contribution he is uniquely expected to make is to give others vision and ability to perform. It is vision and moral responsibility that, in the last analysis, define the manager.' This morality is reflected in the five areas identified by Drucker 'in which practices are required to ensure the right spirit throughout management organization'.

1   There must be high performance requirements; no

condoning of poor or mediocre performance; and rewards must be based on performance.

2   Each management job must be a rewarding job in itself rather than just a step on the promotion ladder.

3   There must be a rational and just promotion system.

4   Management needs a 'charter' spelling out clearly who has the power to make 'life-and-death' decisions affecting a manager; and there should be some way for a manager to appeal to a higher court.

5   In its appointments, management must demonstrate that it realizes that integrity is the one absolute requirement of a manager, the one quality that he has to being with him and cannot be expected to acquire later on.

At the time, the idea from *The Practice of Management* which was seized upon was what became known as Management By Objectives (MBO). 'A manager's job should be based on a task to be performed in order to attain the company's objectives ... the manager should be directed and controlled by the objectives of performance rather than by his boss,' Drucker writes.

Lacking the populist trend to snappy abbreviation, Drucker always refers to 'management by objectives and self control'. Drucker's inspiration for the idea of MBO was Harold Smiddy of General Electric who Drucker knew well. He also acknowledges Alfred Sloan, Pierre DuPont and Donaldson Brown of DuPont as practitioners of MBO.

As MBO became popularized, interpretations became more narrow than that proposed by Drucker. 'The performance that is expected of the manager must be derived from the performance goal of the business, his results must be measured by the contribution they make to the success of the enterprise. The manager must know and understand what the business goals demand of him in terms of performance and his superior must know what contribution to demand and expect of him – and must judge him accordingly,' he writes.

In practice the personal element in Drucker's interpretation of MBO was subsumed by the corporate. Instead of being a pervasive means of understanding, motivation and satisfaction, MBO became a simplistic means of setting a corporate goal and heading towards it.

With its examinations of GM, Ford and others, Drucker's audience and world view in *The Practice of Management* is resolutely that of the large corporation. The world has moved on. In *Liberation Management*, Tom Peters (1992) describes the book as 'one long diatribe against intuition – and one long paean to hyperrational approaches to harnessing large numbers of people in large organizations'. While this is largely true, *The Practice of Management* is critical of overly hierarchical organizations – Drucker recommends seven layers as the maximum necessary for any organization.

Drucker also identifies 'seven new tasks' for the manager of the future. Given that these were laid down over 40 years ago, their prescience is astounding. Drucker writes that tomorrow's managers must:

1   manage by objectives
2   take more risks and for a longer period ahead
3   be able to make strategic decisions
4   be able to built an integrated team, each member of which is capable of managing and of measuring his own performance and results in relation to the common objectives
5   be able to communicate information fast and clearly
6   be able to see the business as a whole and to integrate his function with it – traditionally a manager has been expected to know one or more functions, but this will no longer be enough
7   be knowledgeable – traditionally a manager has been

expected to know a few products or one industry – this, too, will no longer be enough.

In 1973 Drucker re-evaluated some of his conclusions in *Management: Tasks, Responsibilities and Practices*, an equally impressive examination of the role and nature of management. However, *The Practice of Management* remains more complete in that it laid the groundwork for many of the developments in management thinking during the sixties.

Notes

1 'Good guru guide', *The Economist*, 25 December–7 January, 1994.
2 Peter Drucker, salvationist', *The Economist* 1 October, 1994.

13

PETER F. DRUCKER

The Age of Discontinuity

1969

Hamel on Drucker

"Peter Drucker's reputation is as a management theorist. He has also been a management prophet. Writing in 1969 he clearly anticipated the emergence of the 'knowledge economy'. I'd like to set a challenge for would-be management gurus: try to find something to say that Peter Drucker has not said first, and has not said well. This high hurdle should substantially reduce the number of business books clogging the book-shelves of booksellers, and offer managers the hope of gaining some truly fresh insights."

T *he Age of Discontinuity* provides a far reaching insight into the business world which largely now exists in the 1990s. Yet, it is nearly thirty years old. 'Businessmen will have to learn to build and manage innovative organizations,' predicts Peter Drucker in *The Age of Discontinuity* echoing today's familiar refrain from a score of thinkers.

In the years since its publication, the reputation of *The Age of Discontinuity* has steadily increased. It is now widely regarded as a classic. 'I remember reading *The Age of Discontinuity* in 1970,' says Philip Sadler, former head of the UK's Ashridge Management College. 'The lucidity of his historical analysis of the period between 1900 and 1965 put it all in perspective. This insight into the past is combined with astonishingly accurate predictions of the future.'[1] In *Managing on the Edge*, published in 1990, Richard Pascale simply accepts the accuracy of Drucker's insights, commenting: 'Peter Drucker's book *The Age of Discontinuity* describes the commercial era in which we live.'

The idea from *The Age of Discontinuity* which has now gained the widest currency is that of the 'knowledge worker', the highly trained, intelligent managerial professional who realizes his or her own worth and contribution to the organization. (The foundations of this idea can easily be seen in Drucker's description of MBO in *The Practice of Management* where the worth, motivation, and aspirations of the executive are integral to corporate success.)

'The knowledge worker sees himself just as another "professional", no different from the lawyer, the teacher, the preacher, the doctor or the government servant of yesterday,' writes Drucker. 'He has the same education. He has more income, he has probably greater opportunities as well. He may well realize that he depends on the organization for access to income and opportunity, and that without the investment the organization has made – and a high investment at that – there would be no job for him, but he also realizes, and rightly so, that the organization equally depends on him.'

Typically, Drucker points to the social ramifications of this new breed of corporate executive. If knowledge, rather than labor, is the new measure of economic society then the fabric of capitalist society must change: 'The knowledge worker is both the true "capitalist" in the knowledge society and dependent on his job. Collectively the knowledge workers, the employed educated middle-class of today's society, own the means of production through pension funds, investment trusts, and so on. Knowledge is power and ownership.'

Drucker has since developed his thinking on the role of knowledge – most notably in his 1992 book, *Managing for the Future* in which he observes: 'From now on the key is knowledge. The world is becoming not labor intensive, not materials intensive, not energy intensive, but knowledge intensive'.

The Age of Discontinuity is also notable for Drucker's criticisms of business schools – another theme which he has since developed. 'The business schools in the US, set up less than a century ago, have been preparing well-trained clerks,' he writes. More importantly, Drucker introduces the idea of privatization – though he labels it 'reprivatization'. This was energetically seized upon by politicians in the 1980s, though their interpretation of privatization goes far beyond that envisaged by Drucker.

Drucker's discussion of 'reprivatization' has tended to distract attention from the many other far-sighted concepts which he examines and accurately predicts. Discontinuity – in the shape of the oil crisis – was just around the corner and its full implications are only now being explored and slowly appreciated.

Notes
1 Interview with Stuart Crainer, July 30, 1996.

14

HENRI FAYOL

General and Industrial Management

1949[1]

"While modern management theory has had many fathers, and a few mothers, Henri Fayol was the first to conceptualize and articulate the work of the twentieth century manager. His view of the manager as an integrator of functional activities captured the essence of general management. While modern technology, which has dramatically improved communications and reduced organizational 'distance', means that large organizations may be able to get along with fewer managers than in Fayol's day, his general principles of management have proved to be surprisingly timeless. Fayol was Europe's first management guru – a pity that Europe has not produced more of his stature in the last 75 years."

Henri Fayol (1841-1925)

Henri Fayol was educated in Lyon, France and at the National School of Mines in St. Etienne. In 1860 he graduated as a mining engineer and joined the French mining company, Commentry-Fourchamboult-Décazeville. He spent his entire working career with the company and was its managing director between 1888 and 1918. During that time he produced the 'functional principle', the first rational approach to the organization of enterprise. His studies led to lectures at the *Ecole Supérieure de la Guerre* and to an examination of the public services.

The origins of *General and Industrial Management* can be traced back to 1900 when Fayol delivered a speech at a mining conference. When he gave a developed version of his ideas at a 1908 conference, 2,000 copies were immediately reprinted to satisfy demand. By 1925, 15,000 copies had been printed and a book was published.

Igor Ansoff has noted that Fayol 'anticipated imaginatively and soundly most of the more recent analyses of modern business practice'.[2]

hile, across the Atlantic, Frederick Taylor examined the tasks of steel workers, France's Henri Fayol created a system of management encapsulated in *General and Industrial Management*. Indeed, Fayol put management at the center of the organization in a way never envisaged by Taylor. 'Management plays a very important part in the government of undertakings; of all undertakings, large or small, industrial, commercial, political, religious or any other,' he writes.

Fayol's system was based on acceptance of and adherence to different functions (and was later influential on Alfred P. Sloan at General Motors). 'All activities to which industrial undertakings give rise can be divided into the following six groups,' writes Fayol. The six functions which he identifies are:

- technical activities
- commercial activities
- financial activities
- security activities
- accounting activities
- managerial activities.

'The management function is quite distinct from the other five essential functions,' notes Fayol. 'To manage is to forecast and plan, to organize, to command, to co-ordinate and to control.' This brief resume of what constitutes management has largely held sway throughout the twentieth century. Only now, is it being seriously questioned and challenged.

From his observations, Fayol also produces general principles of management:

- division of work
- authority and responsibility
- discipline
- unity of command

- unity of direction
- subordination of individual interest to general interest
- remuneration of personnel
- centralization
- scalar chain (line of authority)
- order
- equity
- stability of tenure of personnel
- initiative
- *esprit de corps.*

Fayol's methods were later exposed by Drucker who observed: 'If used beyond the limits of Fayol's model, functional structure becomes costly in terms of time and effort'.[2] While this is undoubtedly true, Fayol's observations and conclusions are important. He talks of 'ten yearly forecasts ... revised every five years' – one of the first instances of business planning in practice and writes: 'The maxim, "managing means looking ahead", gives some idea of the importance attached to planning in the business world, and it is true that if foresight is not the whole of management at least it is an essential part of it.'

In *The Principles and Practice of Management*, one of the first comprehensive studies of the fledgling years of management thinking, its editor E.F.L. Brech (1953) notes: 'The importance of Fayol's contribution lay in two features: the first was his systematic analysis of the process of management; the second, his form advocacy of the principle that management can, and should, be taught. Both were revolutionary lines of thought in 1908, and still little accepted in 1925.'

Fayol's championing of management was highly important. While Frederick Taylor regarded managers as little more than overseers with limited responsibility, Fayol regarded their role as critical to organizational success. In his faith in carefully defined functions, Fayol was systematizing business organization in ways which worked at the time, but proved too limiting and restraining in the long term.

Notes

1 This book was originally published in French as *Administration Industrielle et Générale* (1916) and first published in English as *General and Industrial Management*, Pitman, London, 1949.
2 Quoted in 'The corporate sages', *Business* September 1988.

15

MARY PARKER FOLLETT

Dynamic Administration

1941

Hamel on Follett

"The work of Mary Parker Follett is refreshingly different from that of her peers. She was the first modern thinker to get us close to the human soul of management. She had the heart of a humanist, not an engineer. One is tempted to wonder how different our understanding of management might be if women like Mary Parker Follett had played a bigger role in the development of modern management theory."

Mary Parker Follett (1868–1933)

Born in Quincy, Massachusetts, **Mary Parker Follett** attended Thayer Academy and the Society for the Collegiate Instruction of Women in Cambridge (now part of Harvard). She spent time at England's Cambridge University and in Paris. Her first published work was *The Speaker of the House of Representatives* (1896) which she wrote while still a student.

Follett's career was largely spent in social work though her books appeared regularly – *The New State: Group Organization – The Solution of Popular Government* (1918), an influential description of Follett's brand of dynamic democracy, and *Creative Experience* (1924), Follett's first business-oriented book. In her later years she was in great demand as a lecturer. After the death of a long-time partner, Isobel Briggs in 1926, she moved to London.

Follett's work was largely neglected in the West, but she was honored in Japan, where there is a Follett Society. Her work has now been brought to a wider audience through the UK academic Pauline Graham – in 1994, Graham edited *Mary Parker Follett: Prophet of Management* a compendium of Follett's writings with commentaries from a host of contemporary figures including Kanter, Drucker and Mintzberg.

M ary Parker Follett's work stands as a humane counterpoint to that of Frederick Taylor and the proponents of Scientific Management. Follett was a female, liberal humanist in an era dominated by reactionary males intent on mechanizing the world of business. 'We should remember that we can never wholly separate the human from the mechanical sides,' warns Follett in *Dynamic Administration*. 'The study of human relations in business and the study of the technology of operating are bound up together.'

During her life, Mary Parker Follett's thinking on management was generally ignored – though in Japan there was a great deal of interest in her perspectives. In her advocacy of human relations she was ahead of her time, something acknowledged by E.F.L. Brech in his book *The Principles and Practice of Management* (1953). 'Mary Follett, broadly, was less interested in the practice of management than in the extent to which the everyday incidents and problems reflected the presence or absence of sound principle. She was chiefly concerned to teach principles in simple language, amply illustrated from everyday events – not the mechanics of management, but its special human character, its nature as a social process, deeply embedded in the emotions of man and in the interrelations to which the everyday working of industry necessarily gives rise – at manager levels, at worker levels, and, of course, between the two,' writes Brech. 'Bearing in mind she was speaking of America in the early 1920s, her thinking can be described as little less than revolutionary, and certainly a generation ahead of its time. There is no evidence that Mary Follett had any contact with the persons who sponsored or conducted the Hawthorne Investigations, but the findings of those investigations, when they appeared in their full form in the 1930s, were a striking testimony to the soundness of her teaching.'

Published eight years after her death, *Dynamic Administration* is a collection of Follett's papers on management gathered from 12 lectures between 1925 and 1933. It includes a great deal of forthright and resoundingly contemporary-sounding comments. 'I think we should undepartmentalize our thinking in regard to every problem that comes to us,' says Follett. 'I do not think that we have psychological and ethical and economic problems. We have human problems, with psychological, ethical and economical aspects, and as many others as you like.'

Follett advocates giving greater responsibility to people – at a time when the mechanical might of mass production was at its height. 'Responsibility is the great developer of men,' she writes. There is also a modern ring to Follett's advice on leadership: 'The most successful leader of all is one who sees another picture not yet actualized.' Follett suggests that a leader is someone who sees the whole rather than the particular, organizes the experiences of the group, offers a vision of the future and trains followers to become leaders. 'Follett sent one principal message: relationships matter,' says Rosabeth Moss Kanter. 'Underpinning all of her work is the importance of relationships, not just transactions, in organizations. She pointed to the reciprocal nature of relationships, the mutual influence developed when people work together, however formal authority is defined.'[1]

In particular, Follett explores conflict. She argues that as conflict is a fact of life 'we should, I think, use it to work for us'. Follett points out three ways of dealing with confrontation: domination, compromise or integration. The latter, she concludes, is the only positive way forward. This can be achieved by first 'uncovering' the real conflict and then taking 'the demands of both sides and breaking them up into their constituent parts'. 'Our outlook is narrowed, our activity is restricted, our chances of business success largely diminished when our thinking is constrained within the limits of what has been called an either-or situation. We should never allow ourselves to be bullied by an "either-or". There is often the possibility of something better than either of two given alternatives,' Follett writes.

To some, Follett remains a Utopian idealist, out of touch with reality; to others, she is a torchbearer of good sense whose ideas have sadly not had significant impact on organizations. 'Integration requires understanding, in-depth understanding,' says Henry Mintzberg. 'It requires serious commitment and dedication. It takes effort, and it depends on creativity. There is precious little of all of these qualities in too many of our organizations today.'

Notes

1 Quoted by Graham, Pauline (editor), in *Mary Parker Follett: Prophet of Management* (1994).

16

HENRY FORD

My Life and Work

1923

Hamel on Ford

"Henry Ford may have been autocratic and paranoid, but he brought to men and women everywhere a stunningly precious gift – mobility. Whatever his faults, Henry Ford was driven by the dream of every great entrepreneur – to make a real difference in people's lives, and to do it globally."

Henry Ford (1863-1947)

After spending time as a machinist's apprentice, a watch repairer and a mechanic, **Henry Ford** built his first car in 1896. Initially, Ford was fascinated by the mechanical possibilities and drove racing cars. Quickly he became convinced of the commercial potential and started his own company in 1899. Through innovative use of new mass production techniques, between 1908 and 1927 Ford produced 15 million Model Ts. In 1919 Ford resigned as the company's President with his son, Edsel, taking over. By then the Ford company was making a car a minute.

M *y Life and Work* was published in Henry Ford's sixtieth year when he bestrode the modern industrial world like a colossus. It is a robust account of his life and business philosophy. Indeed, it is notable for the dominance of the former and the lack of the latter.

Ford's business thinking is simply expressed: 'Our policy is to reduce the price, extend the operations, and improve the article,' he writes. 'You will notice that the reduction of price comes first. We have never considered any costs as fixed. Therefore we first reduce the price to the point where we believe more sales will result. Then we go ahead and try to make the prices. We do not bother about the costs. The new price forces the costs down. The more usual way is to take the costs and then determine the price, and although that method may be scientific in the narrow sense; it is not scientific in the broad sense, because what earthly use is it to know the cost if it tells you that you cannot manufacture at a price at which the article can be sold?' Ford's commitment to lowering prices cannot be doubted. Between 1908 and 1916 he reduced prices by 58 percent – at a time when demand was such that he could easily have raised prices.

The above extract from *My Life and Work* was quoted by Ted Levitt in his article 'Marketing myopia' (1960). In it, he provides an unconventional interpretation of Ford's gifts. 'In a sense Ford was both the most brilliant and the most senseless marketer in American history. He was senseless because he refused to give the customer anything but a black car. He was brilliant because he fashioned a production system designed to fit market needs. We habitually celebrate him for the wrong reason, his production genius. His real genius was marketing ... mass production was the result not the cause of his low prices.'

Ford's masterly piece of marketing lay in his intuitive realization that the mass car market existed – it just remained for him to provide the products the market wanted. In management jargon, Ford stuck to the knitting. Model Ts were black, straightforward and affordable. At the center of Ford's thinking was the aim of standardization – something continually emphasized by the car makers of today though they talk in terms of quality, and Ford in quantity.' I have no use for a motor car which has more spark plugs than a cow has teats,' said Ford. The trouble was that when other manufacturers added extras, Ford kept it simple and dramatically lost ground.

The company's reliance on the Model T nearly drove it to self-destruction even though at one time Ford had cash reserves of $1 billion. Henry Ford is reputed to have kicked a slightly modified Model T to pieces such was his commitment to the unadulterated version. The man with a genius for marketing lost touch with the aspirations of customers.

More conventionally, Ford is celebrated – if that is the right word – for his transformation of the production line into a means of previously unimagined mass production. Production, in the Ford company's huge plant, was based round strict functional divides – demarcations. Ford believed in people getting on with their jobs and not raising their heads above functional parapets. He did not want engineers talking to salespeople, or people making decisions without his approval.

In *My Life and Work* Ford gives a chilling insight into his own unforgiving logic. He calculates that the production of a Model T requires over 8,000 different operations. Of these 949 require 'strong, able-bodied, and practically physically perfect men' and 3,338 require 'ordinary physical strength'. The remainder, says Ford, could be undertaken by 'women or older children' and 'we found that 670 could be filled by legless men, 2,637 by one-legged men, two by armless men, 715 by one-armed men and 10 by blind men'.

With characteristic forthrightness, management and managers were dismissed by Ford as largely unnecessary. 'Fundamental to Henry Ford's misrule was a systematic, deliberate and conscious attempt to run the billion-dollar business without managers. The secret police that spied on all Ford executives served to inform Henry Ford of any attempt on the part of one of his executives to make a decision,' noted Peter Drucker in *The Practice of Management* (1954). Ford's lack of faith in management proved the undoing of the huge corporate empire he assembled. Without his autocratic belligerence to drive the company forward, it quickly ground to a halt.

Even so, Ford's achievements are not in doubt. 'In some respects Ford remains a good role model,' says Ray Wild, principal of Henley Management College. 'He was an improviser and innovator, he borrowed ideas and then adapted and synthesized them. He developed flow lines that involved people; now, we have flow lines without people, but no-one questions their relevance or importance. Though he is seen as having de-humanized work, it shouldn't be forgotten that he provided a level of wealth for workers and products for consumers which weren't previously available.' Among his many innovations was a single human one: Ford introduced the $5 wage for his workers which, at that time, was around twice the average for the industry.

Ford will never be celebrated for his humanity or people management skills. But, in the realms of business, he had an international perspective which was ahead of his time. His plant at Highland Park, Detroit, produced – the world, not just the US, bought. Also, Ford was acutely aware that time was an important competitive weapon – 'Time waste differs from material waste in that there can be no salvage,' he observed. Ford's business achievements and contribution to the development of industrialization are likely to be remembered long after his theories on politics, history, motivation or humanity.

17

MICHAEL GOOLD,
MARCUS ALEXANDER &
ANDREW CAMPBELL

Corporate-Level Strategy

1994

Hamel on Goold et al.

"Chandler and Drucker celebrated large multi-divisional organizations, but as these companies grew, decentralized and diversified, the corporate center often became little more than a layer of accounting consolidation. In the worst cases, a conglomerate was worth less than its break-up value, and the difference between unit strategy and corporate strategy was a stapler. In writing the definitive book on corporate strategy, Goold, Alexander and Campbell gave hope to corporate bureaucrats everywhere. Maybe, occasionally, it really was possible for the corporate level to add value."

Michael Goold, Andrew Campbell & Marcus Alexander

Michael Goold, Andrew Campbell and **Marcus Alexander** are directors of the Ashridge Strategic Management Centre, London, England. They were previously strategy consultants with either the Boston Consulting Group or McKinsey & Company.

Michael Goold and Andrew Campbell are the authors of the highly influential *Strategies and Styles* (1987). Among the group's other books are *Managing the Multibusiness Company* (Goold and Kathleen Sommers Luchs, 1995); *Strategic Synergy* (Campbell and Luchs, 1992); *Strategic Control* (Goold with John J. Quinn, 1990); and *Break Up!* (Campbell and Richard Koch, 1996).

T he basic, and accurate, realization behind Michael Goold, Marcus Alexander and Andrew Campbell's *Corporate-Level Strategy* is that most large companies are now multibusiness organizations. The logic behind this fact of business life is one which is generally assumed rather than examined in any depth. Multibusiness companies through their very size offer economies of scale and synergies between the various businesses which can be exploited to the overall good.

While this is a truth universally acknowledged, Goold, Campbell and Alexander's research suggests that this *raison d'être* does not, in reality, exist. They calculate that in over half multibusiness companies the whole is worth less than the sum of its parts. Instead of adding and nurturing value, the corporation actually negates value. It is costly and its influence, though pervasive, is often counter-productive.

This condemnation is not restricted to what we would normally consider to be conglomerates. Goold, Campbell and Alexander suggest that the baleful influence of the corporate parent also applies to companies with portfolios in a single industry, or in a series of apparently related areas.

One of the primary causes of this phenomena is that while the individual businesses within the organization often have strategies, the corporation as a whole does not. They may pretend otherwise, but the proclaimed strategy is often an amalgam of the individual business strategies given credence by general aspirations.

If corporate level strategy is to add value, Goold, Campbell and Alexander suggest that there needs to be a tight fit between the parent organization and its businesses. Successful corporate parents focus on a narrow range of tasks and create value in those areas, and align the structures, processes and central functions of the parent accordingly. Rather than all-encompassing and constantly interfering, the center is akin to a specialist medical practitioner – intervening in its areas of expertise when it knows it can suggest a cure.

From their detailed analysis of 15 successful multi-business corporations, Goold, Campbell and Alexander identify three essentials to successful corporate strategies. First, there must be a clear insight about the role of the parent. If the parent does not know how or where it can add value it is unlikely to do so. Second, the parent must have distinctive characteristics. They, too, have a corporate culture and personality. Third, there must be recognition that 'each parent will only be effective with certain sorts of business' – described as their 'heartland'.

'Heartland businesses are also well understood by the parent; they do not suffer from the inappropriate influence and meddling that can damage less familiar businesses. The parent has an innate feel for its heartland that enables it to make difficult judgments and decisions with a high degree of success,' say the authors. Heartlands are broad ranging and can cover different industries, markets and technologies. Given this added complexity, the ability of the parent to intervene on a limited number of issues is crucial.

The concept of heartland businesses is, they make clear, distinct from core businesses. Though core businesses may be important and substantial, say Goold, Campbell and Alexander, the parent may not be adding a great deal to them. 'A core business is often merely a business that the company has decided to commit itself to,' they write. 'In contrast, the heartland definition focuses on the **fit** between a parent and a business: do the parent's insights and behavior fit the opportunities and nature of this business? Does the parent have specialist skills in assisting this type of business to perform better?'

Corporate strategy should be driven by, what Goold, Campbell and Alexander label, 'parenting advantage' – 'to create more value in the portfolio of businesses than would be achieved by any rival'. To do so, requires a fundamental change in basic perspectives on the role of the parent and of the nature of the multibusiness organization.

'Anyone who reads *Corporate-Level Strategy* will subsequently think and talk about corporate strategy in a different way,' noted Bain & Company's Robin Buchanan, adding, 'It is to be hoped that they will act on it, too.'[1]

Note

1 Buchanan, Robin, 'Practical Parenting', *The Observer*, October 23, 1994.

18

GARY HAMEL & C.K. PRAHALAD

Competing for the Future

1994

Hamel on Hamel & C.K. Prahalad

"By the 1990s strategy had become discredited. All too often 'vision' was ego masquerading as foresight; planning was formulaic, incrementalist and largely a waste of time in a world of discontinuous change; 'strategic' investments were those that lost millions, if not billions of dollars. In practice, strategy development too often started with the past, rather than with the future. As strategy professors, CK and I had a simple choice: change jobs or try to reinvent strategy for a new age. We chose the latter course. We'll let you judge whether we succeeded."

Gary Hamel & C.K. Prahalad

C.K. Prahalad is Harvey C. Fruehauf Professor of Business Administration at the University of Michigan's Graduate School of Business Administration. He is co-author, with INSEAD's Yves Doz, of *The Multinational Mission: Balancing Local Responsiveness and Global Vision* and is a consultant to many leading firms including AT&T, Motorola and Philips.

Gary Hamel is Visiting Professor of Strategic and International Management at London Business School. Based in Woodside, California, he is a consultant to major companies including EDS, Nokia and Dow, and Chairman of Strategos, a worldwide strategic consulting company.

Hamel and Prahalad's articles 'Strategic intent' and 'Competing with core competencies' won McKinsey awards in the *Harvard Business Review*. Their article 'The core competence of the corporation' is one of the most reprinted articles in the *Review's* history.

T he debate on the meaning and application of strategy is long running. Each decade produces its own interpretation and its own voice. The 1960s gave us the resolutely analytical Igor Ansoff; the 1970s Henry Mintzberg and his cerebral and creative 'crafting strategy'; the 1980s, Michael Porter's rational route to competitiveness, and nominations for the leading strategic thinkers of the 1990s would certainly short-list Gary Hamel and C.K. Prahalad.

Gary Hamel and C.K. Prahalad's *Competing for the Future* has been seized on as the blueprint for a new generation of strategic thinking. *Business Week* named it as the best management book of 1994 and it has sold over 250,000 copies in hardcover. 'At a time when many companies continue to lay off thousands in massive reengineering exercises, this is a book that deserves widespread attention,' observed *Business Week's* John Byrne (1994). 'It's a valuable and worthwhile tonic for devotees of today's slash-and-burn school of management.'

Hamel and Prahalad believe strategy has tied itself into a straitjacket of narrow, and narrowing, perspectives: 'Among the people who work on strategy in organizations and the theorists, a huge proportion, perhaps 95 percent, are economists and engineers who share a mechanistic view of strategy. Where are the theologists, the anthropologists to give broader and fresher insights?'

They argue that strategy is multi-faceted, emotional as well as analytical, concerned with meaning, purpose and passion. While strategy is a process of learning and discovery, it is not looked on as a learning process and this represents a huge blind spot.

Broader perspectives are necessitated by the 'emerging competitive reality' in which the onus is on transforming not just individual organizations but entire industries. The boldness of such objectives is put in perspective when Hamel and Prahalad observe that, for all the research and books on the subject, there remains no theory of strategy creation. Strategy emerges and the real problem, executives perceive, is not creating strategy but in implementing it.

'We have an enormous appetite for simplicity. We like to believe we can break strategy down to Five Forces or Seven Ss. But you can't. Strategy is extraordinarily emotional and demanding. It is not a ritual or a once-a-year exercise, though that is what it has become. We have set the bar too low,' say Hamel and Prahalad. As a result, managers are bogged down in the nitty-gritty of the present – spending less than three percent of their time looking to the future.

Instead of talking about strategy or planning, they advocate that companies should talk of *strategizing* and ask 'What are the fundamental preconditions for developing complex, variegated, robust strategies?' Strategizing is part of the new managerial argot of 'strategic intent', 'strategic architecture', 'foresight' (rather than vision) and, crucially, the idea of 'core competencies'.

Hamel and Prahalad define core competencies as 'the collective learning in the organization, especially how to co-ordinate diverse production skills and integrate multiple streams of technologies' and call on organizations to see themselves as a portfolio of core competencies as opposed to business units. The former are geared to growing 'opportunity share' wherever that may be; the latter narrowly focused on market share and more of the same.

The surge of interest in core competencies has tended to enthusiastic over simplification. 'You need to be cautious about where core competencies will lead you,' warns Marcus Alexander of the Ashridge Strategic Management Centre during an interview in 1996. 'They are a very powerful weapon in some cases but are not the sole basis for a sound corporate strategy. They can encourage companies to get into businesses simply because they see a link between core competencies rather than ones where they have an in-depth knowledge. Similarly, there is a temptation for mature companies to be persuaded to go into growth businesses when that is not necessarily the best option for them.'

In some ways, Hamel and Prahalad's strategic prognosis falls between two extremes. At one extreme are the arch-rationalists, insisting on a constant stream of data to support any strategy; at the other are the 'thriving on chaos' school with their belief in free-wheeling organizations where strategy is a moveable feast.

There is a thin dividing line between order and chaos. 'Neither Stalinist bureaucracy nor Silicon Valley provide an optimal economic system,' they caution. 'Silicon Valley is extraordinarily good at creating new ideas but in other ways is extraordinarily inefficient. There are 100 failures for every success and, in fact, you find that smaller companies usually succeed in partnership with large organizations.'

They conclude that small entrepreneurial off-shoots are not the route to organizational regeneration. They are too random, inefficient and prone to becoming becalmed by corporate indifference. This does not mean that interlopers cannot change the shape of entire industries.

In Europe, they acknowledge the revolutionary impact of entrepreneurial newcomers such as IKEA, Body Shop, Swatch and Virgin. But, the true challenge is to create revolutions when you are large and dominant. This is something which American companies – such as Motorola and Hewlett-Packard – are more successful at than their European counterparts.

This is partly attributable to traditional cultures. 'We are moving to more democratic models of organization to which US corporations appear more attuned. In Europe and Japan there is a much more elitist sense that all knowledge resides at the top. There is a hierarchy of experience, not a hierarchy of imagination. And the half life of experience is very short.'

The two are also long-standing critics of the corporate obsession with downsizing, labeling it 'corporate anorexia'. The golden rules are summed up by Hamel and Prahalad: 'A company surrenders today's businesses when it gets smaller faster than it gets better. A company surrenders tomorrow's businesses when it gets better without getting different.' Downsizing is an easy option – 'There is nothing more short-term than a sixty-year-old CEO holding a fist full of share options'.

Growth (they prefer to talk of vitality) comes from difference; though they add the caveat that 'there are as many stupid ways to grow as there are to downsize. You might merge with another organization but two drunks don't make a sensible person'. The catch-22 for organizations is that vitality is usually ignited by a crisis – something borne out by the burgeoning literature on spectacular turnarounds.

Perhaps reassuringly, Hamel and Prahalad believe vitality comes from within. If only executives would listen – 'Go to any company and ask when was the last time someone in their twenties spent time with the board teaching them something they didn't know. For many it is inconceivable, yet companies will pay millions of dollars for the opinions of McKinsey's bright 29-year-old. What about their own 29-year-olds?'

While such questions remain largely unanswered, Hamel and Prahalad are moving on to pose yet more: 'Something new needed to be said about the content of strategy. Now we need to rethink the process of strategy.'

19

CHARLES HANDY

The Age of Unreason

1989

Hamel on Handy

❝There is no contemporary management thinker who is more genuinely, and originally, thoughtful than Charles Handy. Charles is one of the few management writers who can step entirely outside the world of management and then look back in. This outside–in perspective yields an uncompromising and unorthodox perspective which will discomfort and enlighten anyone who cares about the future of management and organizations. Where most business authors are intent on giving you the 'how', Professor Handy forces us to ask 'why?'.**❞**

Charles Handy

Charles Handy (born 1932) is a writer and broadcaster. Irish-born, he worked for Shell before joining academia. He spent time at MIT and later joined London Business School.

His first book belies the wide ranging, social and philosophical nature of his later work. *Understanding Organizations* (1976) is a comprehensive and readable primer of organizational theory. It is the most conventional of his books. Its sequel was the idiosyncratic *Gods of Management* (1978).

Over the last decade Handy has sealed his reputation as a thinker. His books routinely crop up in bestseller lists and he has spread his wings to become a much-quoted sage on the future of society and work. His articles are as likely to appear in the *Harvard Business Review* as in the lifestyle sections of tabloid newspapers. The cornerstones of his ideas on emerging working structures can be found in *The Age of Unreason* and his 1994 bestseller *The Empty Raincoat* (called *The Age of Paradox* in the United States).

C harles Handy's *The Age of Unreason* is a disquieting book – and remains so years after its publication. The age of unreason, which Handy predicts, is 'a time when what we used to take for granted may no longer hold true, when the future, in so many areas, is there to be shaped, by us and for us; a time when the only prediction that will hold true is that no predictions will hold. A time, therefore, for bold imagings in private life as well as public, for thinking the unlikely and doing the unreasonable.'

The future, writes Handy, will be one of 'discontinuous change' (a phrase which has now entered the mainstream). The path through time, with society slowly, naturally and radically improving on a steady course, is a thing of the past. The blinkers have to be removed. Handy tells the story of the Peruvian Indians who saw invading ships on the horizon. Having no knowledge of such things, they discounted them as a freak of the weather. They settled for their sense of continuity.

In order to adapt to a society in which mysterious invaders are perpetually on the horizon, the way people think will have to change fundamentally. 'We are all prisoners of our past. It is hard to think of things except in the way we have always thought of them. But that solves no problems and seldom changes anything,' writes Handy. He points out that people who have thought unconventionally, 'unreasonably', have had the most profound impact on twentieth-century living. Freud, Marx and Einstein succeeded through 'discontinuous' (or what Handy labels 'upside down') thinking.

He sees the need for the development of 'a new intelligentsia'. Education will have to alter radically as the way people think can only be changed by revolutionizing the way they learn and think about learning,

In practice, Handy believes that certain forms of organization will become dominant. These are the type of organization most readily associated with service industries. First, what he calls 'the shamrock organization' – 'a form of organization based around a core of essential executives and workers supported by outside contractors and part-time help'. The consequence of such an organizational form is that organizations in the future are likely to resemble the way consultancy firms, advertising agencies and professional partnerships are currently structured.

The second emergent structure identified by Handy is the federal one. It is not, he points out, another word for decentralization. He provides a blueprint for federal organizations in which the central function coordinates, influences, advises and suggests. It does not dictate terms or short-term decisions. The center is, however, concerned with long-term strategy. It is 'at the middle of things and is not a polite word for the top or even for head office'. (Handy develops his federal thinking in *The Empty Raincoat*.)

The third type of organization Handy anticipates is what he calls 'the Triple I'. The three 'Is' are information, intelligence and ideas. In such organizations the demands on personnel management are large. Explains Handy: 'The wise organization already knows that their smart people are not to be easily defined as workers or as managers but as individuals, as specialist, as professional or executives, or as leader (the older terms of manager and worker are dropping out of use), and that they and it need also to be obsessed with the pursuit of learning if they are going to keep up with the pace of change.'

Discontinuity demands new organizations, new people to run them with new skills, capacities and career patterns. No one will be able to work simply as a manager; organizations will demand much more,

As organizations will change in the age of unreason so, Handy predicts, will other aspects of our lives. Less time will be spent at work – 50,000 hours in a lifetime rather than the present figure of around 100,000. Handy does not predict, as people did in the 1970s, an enlightened age of leisure. Instead he challenges people to spend more time thinking about what they want to do, Time will not simply be divided between work and play – there could be 'portfolios' which split time between fee work (where you sell time); gift work (for neighbors or charities); study (keeping up-to-date with your work) and homework and leisure.

'An age of unreason is an age of opportunity even if it looks at first sight like the end of all ages,' says Handy. People must seize the opportunity, not ignore the invaders on the horizon.

20

FREDERICK HERZBERG

The Motivation to Work

1959

Hamel on Herzberg

"Pay-for-performance, employee stock owner-ship plans, end-of-year bonuses – too many organizations seem to believe that the only motivation to work is an economic one. Treating knowledge assets like Skinnerian rats is hardly the way to get the best out of people. Herzberg offered a substantially more subtle approach – one that still has much to recommend it. The next time you hear the glib phrase 'people are our most important asset' roll off the tongue of an executive who still regards people as a variable cost, dig out a copy of *The Motivation to Work* and suggest a little bed-time reading.**"**

Frederick Herzberg

Frederick Herzberg (born 1923) served in World War Two and was posted to Dachau concentration camp after its liberation. This proved a powerful experience. On his return to the US, Herzberg studied at the University of Pittsburgh and worked for the US Public Health Service in his area of expertise, clinical psychology.

Along with Maslow and McGregor, he was identified with the Human Relations School of the 1950s. His most influential publication was an article in the *Harvard Business Review* in 1968. 'One More Time: How Do You Motivate Employees?' has sold over one million copies in reprints making it the *Review's* most popular article ever. The article introduced the acronym KITA (kick in the ass) and argued: 'If you have someone on a job, use him. If you can't use him get rid of him.' Herzberg also coined the, now popular, phrase 'job enrichment'. He believes that business organizations could be an enormous force for good, provided they liberate both themselves and their people from the thrall of numbers, and get on with creative expansion of individuals' roles within them.

Herzberg is now Professor of Management at the University of Utah. His co-authors for *The Motivation to Work* were his co-researchers Mausner and Snyderman.

R esearching *The Motivation to Work* Frederick Herzberg and his co-authors, Mausner and Snyderman, asked 203 Pittsburgh engineers and accountants about their jobs and what pleased and displeased them.

As a result, Herzberg separates the motivational elements of work into two categories – those serving people's animal needs (hygiene factors) and those meeting uniquely human needs (motivational factors). In *The Motivation to Work*, Herzberg and his co-authors write: 'Hygiene operates to remove health hazards from the environment of man. It is not a curative; it is, rather, a preventative ... Similarly, when there are deleterious factors in the context of the job, they serve to bring about poor job attitudes. Improvements in these factors of hygiene will serve to remove the impediments to positive job attitudes.'

Hygiene factors – also labeled maintenance factors – are determined to include supervision, inter-personal relations, physical working conditions, salary, company policies and administrative practices, benefits and job security. 'When these factors deteriorate to a level below that which the employee considers acceptable, then job dissatisfaction ensues,' observes Herzberg. Hygiene alone is insufficient to provide the 'motivation to work'. Indeed, the book argues that the factors which provide satisfaction are quite different from those leading to dissatisfaction.

True motivation, says Herzberg, comes from achievement, personal development, job satisfaction and recognition. The aim should be to motivate people through the job itself rather than through rewards or pressure.

Herzberg went on to broaden his research base. This further confirmed his conclusion that hygiene factors are the principle creator of unhappiness in work and motivational factors the route to satisfaction.

Herzberg's work has had a considerable effect on the rewards and remuneration packages offered by corporations.

Increasingly, there is a trend towards 'cafeteria' benefits in which people can choose from a range of options. In effect, they can select the elements which they recognize as providing their own motivation to work.

Similarly, the current emphasis on self-development, career management and self-managed learning can be seen as having evolved from Herzberg's insights. Ultimately, motivation comes from within the individual rather than being created by the organization according to some formula.

21

JOSEPH M. JURAN

Planning for Quality

1988

Hamel on Juran

"A senior executive at an American car company once told me that the company had just finished its twentieth annual study of Toyota. After 20 years, was the company still learning something new about its adversary, I asked. The answer was illuminating. 'For the first five years,' the American manager replied, 'we thought we had a data problem. No one's quality could be that good. For the next five years, we thought it must have something to do with being Japanese – docile workers, group-ism and so on. For the next five years we thought it must be their technology – robots, supply systems, etc. Only in the last five years have we come to realize that they have a fundamentally different philosophy about customers and workers.' The impact of Juran, and of Deming as well, went far beyond quality. By drawing the attention of Western managers to the successes of Japan, they forced Western managers to challenge some of their most basic beliefs about the capabilities of their employees and the expectations of their customers."

Joseph M. Juran

The Romanian-born **Joseph M. Juran** – with W. Edwards Deming – was instigator of the Japanese discovery of quality after the end of World War Two. Born in 1904, Juran is an American electrical engineer who worked for Western Electric in the 1920s and then AT&T. In 1953 he arrived in Tokyo, by which time Deming was already making waves with his quality philosophy. At the invitation of the Japanese Federation of Economic Associations and the Japanese Union of Scientists and Engineers, Juran was asked to spend two months analyzing Japanese approaches to quality.

From his experience, Juran believed Japan's success was built on quality products. This message was ignored as Western businesses continued with their, by then mistaken, belief that Japan was succeeding through lower prices and nothing else. In the 1960s Juran could be found attempting to awaken US executives to the emergence of Japan.

With the 'discovery' of quality in the 1980s, Juran and his work through the Juran Institute came to greater prominence – while remaining slightly in the shadow of Deming. Juran's weighty *Quality Control Handbook* was published in 1951. Juran was awarded the Second Class Order of the Sacred Treasure by the Emperor of Japan – the highest honor for a non-Japanese citizen – for 'the development of quality control in Japan and the facilitation of US and Japanese friendship'.

T alking to Japanese audiences in the 1950s, Joseph Juran's message was enthusiastically absorbed by groups of senior managers. In the West, his audiences were made up of engineers and quality inspectors. Therein, argues Juran, lies the problem. While the Japanese have made quality a priority at the top of the organization, in the West it is delegated downwards, an operational rather than a managerial issue.

In the post-war years, Juran believes US businesses were caught unawares because of two reasons: they assumed their Asian adversaries were copycats rather than innovators, and their chief executives were too obsessed with financial indicators to notice any danger signs.

Juran's quality philosophy, laid out in *Planning for Quality* and his other books, is built around a quality trilogy: quality planning, quality management and quality implementation. While Juran is critical of Deming as being overly reliant on statistics, his own approach is based on the forbiddingly entitled Company-Wide Quality Management (CWQM) which aims to create a means of disseminating quality to all.

Juran insists that quality cannot be delegated and wa an early exponent of what has come to be known as empowerment: for him quality has to be the goal of each employee, individually and in teams, through self-supervision. His approach is less mechanistic than Deming and places greater stress on human relations (though Deming adherents disagree with this interpretation).

Juran places quality in a historical perspective. Manufacturing products to design specifications and then inspecting them for defects to protect the buyer, he points out, was something the Egyptians had mastered 5,000 years previously when building the pyramids. Similarly, the ancient Chinese had set up a separate department of the central government to establish quality standards and maintain them. Juran's message – encapsulated in *Planning for Quality* – is that quality is nothing new. This is a simple, but daunting message. If quality is so elemental and elementary why had it become ignored in the West? Juran's unwillingness to gild his straightforward message is attractive to some, but has made the communication of his ideas less successful than he would have liked.

Where Juran is innovative is in his belief that there is more to quality than specification and rigorous testing for defects. The human side of quality is regarded as critical. The origins of Juran's thoughts can be traced to his time at Western Electric. Juran analyzed the large number of tiny circuit breakers routinely scrapped by the company. Instead of waiting at the end of a production line to count the defective products, Juran looked at the manufacturing process as a whole. He came up with a solution and offered it to his bosses. They were not impressed and told Juran that this was not his job: 'We're the inspection department and our job is to look at these things after they are made and find the bad ones. Making them right in the first place is the job of the production department.'

In response, Juran developed his all-embracing theories of what quality should entail. 'In broad terms, quality planning consists of developing the products and processes required to meet the customers' needs. More specifically, quality planning comprises the following basic activities:

- identify the customers and their needs
- develop a product that responds to those needs
- develop a process able to produce that product.'

Quality planning, says Juran, can be produced through 'a road map ... an invariable sequence of steps'. These are:

- identify who are the customers
- determine the needs of those customers
- translate those needs into our language

- develop a product that can respond to those needs
- optimize the product features so as to meet our needs as well as customers' needs
- develop a process which is able to produce the product
- optimize the process
- prove that the process can produce the product under operating conditions
- transfer the process to the operating forces.

As with so many other recipes for quality, Juran's is more far reaching and difficult to achieve than a list of bullet points can ever suggest.

22

ROSABETH MOSS KANTER

The Change Masters

1983

Hamel on Kanter

"In a turbulent and inhospitable world, corporate vitality is a fragile thing. Yesterday's industry challengers are today's laggards. Entropy is endemic. Certainly *The Change Masters* is the most carefully researched, and best argued, book on change and transformation to date. While Rosabeth may not have discovered the eternal fountain of corporate vitality, she certainly points us in its general direction."

Rosabeth Moss Kanter

Rosabeth Moss Kanter was born in 1943. She graduated from Bryn Mawr and has a Ph.D. from the University of Michigan. After a spell as associate professor at Brandeis University, she joined Harvard's Organization Behavior program in 1978. She has also worked at Yale and MIT and is now a Harvard professor. She is the former editor of the *Harvard Business Review* (1989–92).

Rosabeth Moss Kanter began her career as a sociologist before the transformation into international business guru. In this early period she examined utopian communities and in *Men and Women of the Corporation* (1977) looked at the innermost working of an organization. It was a premature epitaph for corporate man and corporate America before downsizing and technology hit home. 'Kanter-the-guru still studies her subject with a sociologist's eye, treating the corporation not so much as a micro-economy, concerned with turning inputs into outputs, but as a mini-society, bent on shaping individuals to collective ends,' says *The Economist.*[1]

She is co-founder of the Boston-based consultancy firm Goodmeasure. Her more recent books, *When Giants Learn to Dance* (1989) and *World Class: Thriving locally in the global economy* (1995) have cemented her already secure reputation. The sociologist within Kanter remains strong. 'I think we're going to see multinationals playing a very different role, needing to be good corporate citizens because the regions in which they operate will draw them into a wider range of activities,' she predicts.[2]

osabeth Moss Kanter's *The Change Masters* has been dubbed the 'thinking man's *In Search of Excellence*'. *The Change Masters* also became a bestseller, but comparisons with Peters and Waterman's opus are largely futile. (Indeed, the authoritative *Sloan Management Review* concluded it was 'of immeasurably higher quality than such competitors as Peters and Waterman's best-selling *In Search of Excellence*'.) Kanter's analysis of 'corporate entrepreneurs at work' is thoroughly academic. Its prose is slow and occasionally cumbersome, its references lengthy and intricate. It oozes authority.

Kanter defines change masters as 'those people and organizations adept at the art of anticipating the need for, and of leading, productive change'. At the opposite end to the change masters are the 'change resisters' intent on reining in innovation.

The starting point of Kanter's research was a request to 65 vice-presidents of human resources in large companies to name companies which were 'progressive and forward thinking in their systems and practices with respect to people'. Forty-seven companies emerged as leaders in the field. They were then compared to similar companies. The companies with a commitment to human resources were 'significantly higher in long-term profitability and financial growth'. The message is that if you manage your people well, you are probably managing your business well.

The book's sub-title is 'Innovation and entrepreneurship in the American corporation'. Innovation is identified by Kanter as the key to future growth; and the key to developing and sustaining innovation is, says Kanter, an 'integrative' approach rather than a 'segmentalist' one. American woes are firmly placed at the door of 'the quiet suffocation of the entrepreneurial spirit in segmentalist companies'.

'Three new sets of skills are required to manage effectively in such integrative, innovation-stimulating environments,' writes Kanter. 'First are "power skills" – skills in persuading others to invest information, support, and resources in new initiatives driven by an "entrepreneur". Second is the ability to manage the problems associated with the greater use of teams and employee participation. And third is an understanding of how change is designed and constructed in an organization – how the microchanges introduced by individual innovators relate to macrochanges or strategic reorientations.'

Kanter, through *The Change Masters* and her follow-up *When Giants Learn to Dance*, was partly responsible for the rise in interest – if not the practice – of empowerment. (In *The Change Masters* empowerment had yet to be added to the management vocabulary and is not even listed in the index – participation, however, gains a lengthy list of references.) People are put at center stage – 'The degree to which the opportunity to use power effectively is granted to or withheld from individuals is one operative difference between those companies which stagnate and those which innovate'.

In this sense, Kanter's work forms a contemporary development from the Human Relations School of the late 1950s and 1960s. 'Above all, Ms Kanter is too quick to assume that "people-sensitive" strategies must also be "growth-boosting" ones. The most salient fact about the past decade is not the camaraderie of brown-bag lunches, but the epidemic of downsizing,' observed the *Economist* in a profile of Kanter's work.[3]

To Kanter, the addiction to downsizing and continual cuts, is proof that the need for innovation, outlined in *The Change Masters*, is as great as ever.

Notes

1 'Moss Kanter, corporate sociologist', *The Economist*, 15 October, 1994.
2 Quoted in Dickson, Tim, 'An interview with Rosabeth Moss Kanter', *Financial Times*, 17 May, 1996.
3 *The Economist*, op. cit.

23

PHILIP KOTLER

Marketing Management: Analysis, Planning, Implementation and Control

1967

Hamel on Kotler

"There are few MBA graduates alive who have not plowed through Kotler's encyclopedic textbook on marketing, and have not benefited enormously from doing so. I know of no other business author who covers his (or her) territory with such comprehensiveness, clarity and authority as Phil Kotler. I can think of few other books, even within the vaunted company of this volume, whose insights would be of more practical benefit to the average company than those found in *Marketing Management*."

Philip Kotler

Philip Kotler is the S.C. Johnson Distinguished Professor of International Marketing at the J.L. Kellogg Graduate School of Management, Northwestern University. Kotler is one of the leading authorities on marketing. He received his master's degree from the University of Chicago and has a Ph.D. from MIT – both in economics. He has worked at Harvard, where he studied mathematics as a postdoctoral student, and at the University of Chicago where he worked on behavioral science.

He is a prolific author. As well as *Marketing Management: Analysis, Planning, Implementation and Control*, the most widely used marketing book in business schools, his books include *Principles of Marketing: Marketing Models*; *Strategic Marketing for Non-Profit Organizations*; *The New Competition* and *High Visibility*; *Social Marketing: Strategies for Changing Public Behavior* and *Marketing Places*.

An advertisement for a Philip Kotler seminar features four neat aphorisms by way of a summary of marketing in the 1990s: 'Companies pay too much attention to the cost of doing something. They should worry more about the cost of not doing it'; 'Every company should work hard to obsolete its own product line ... before its competitors do'; 'Your company does not belong in any market where it can't be the best'; and 'Marketing takes a day to learn. Unfortunately it takes a life time to master'.

Such observations distill Kotler's massive productiveness down to a few memorable phrases. This is grossly unrepresentative. Kotler's books are text books in the best sense and *Marketing Management* the definitive marketing textbook of our times. It is now in its eighth edition.

Marketing Management is tightly argued and all-encompassing. Through its various editions, its content has been expanded and brought up-to-date. The emerging challenge to all those involved in marketing is potently mapped out by Kotler in the eighth edition, published in 1994. 'The marketing discipline is redeveloping its assumptions, concepts, skills, tools, and systems for making sound business decisions,' writes Kotler. 'Marketers must know when to cultivate large markets and when to niche; when to launch new brands and when to extend existing brand names; when to push products through distribution and when to pull them through distribution; when to protect the domestic market and when to penetrate aggressively into foreign markets; when to add more benefits to the offer and when to reduce the price; and when to expand and when to contract their budgets for salesforce, advertising, and other marketing tools.' The scope of marketing is expanding exponentially as is demonstrated by the size and scope of *Marketing Management* – its contents range from industry and competitor analysis to designing strategies for the global marketplace, from managing product life cycle strategies to retailing, wholesaling and physical distribution systems.

Kotler examines the shift in emphasis from 'transaction oriented' marketing to 'relationship marketing'. 'Good customers are an asset which, when well managed and served, will return a handsome lifetime income stream to the company. In the intensely competitive marketplace, the company's first order of business is to retain customer loyalty through continually satisfying their needs in a superior way,' says Kotler.

For the aspiring or practicing marketer, the attraction of *Marketing Management* lies in the clarity of its definitions of key phrases and roles. It defines marketing as 'a social and managerial process by which individuals and groups obtain what they need and want through creating, offering, and exchanging products of value with others'. Kotler goes on to explain the concept of a market as consisting 'of all the potential customers sharing a particular need or want who might be willing and able to engage in exchange to satisfy that need or want'. Marketing management, therefore, 'is the process of planning and executing the conception, pricing, promotion, and distribution of goods, services, and ideas to create exchanges with target groups that satisfy customer and organizational objectives'.

The clarity of *Marketing Management* enables Kotler to return to the fundamentals. His examination of what makes up a product is typical. Kotler defines a product as 'anything that can be offered to a market for attention, acquisition, use, or consumption that might satisfy a want or need'. He says that a product has five levels: the core benefit ('Marketers must see themselves as benefit providers'); the generic product; the expected product (the normal expectations the customer has of the product); the augmented product (the additional services or benefits added to the product) and, finally, the potential product ('all of the augmentations and transformations that this product might ultimately undergo in the future').

Kotler explores what he labels 'customer delivered value'

which he defines as 'the difference between total customer value and total customer cost. And total customer value is the bundle of benefits customers expect from a given product or service'. Total customer value is made up of product value, service value, personnel value and image value. Total customer cost is made up of monetary price, time cost, energy cost and psychic cost. The two are combined to produce customer delivered value.

Given the scale and challenge of modern marketing outlined by Kotler, it is perhaps little wonder that he laments that so few companies are actually adept and committed to marketing. His list of successful marketing organizations is notable for its brevity. In the United States he identifies Procter & Gamble, Apple, Disney, Nordstrom, Wal-Mart, Milliken, McDonald's, Marriott Hotels and Delta Airlines as true marketing organizations. Elsewhere, the list is even shorter. In Europe, Kotler highlights IKEA, Club Med, Ericsson, Bang & Olufsen and Marks & Spencer and, in Japan, only Sony, Toyota and Canon.

In order to become marketing-oriented, Kotler believes organizations encounter three common hurdles:

1 **Organized resistance** – entrenched functional behavior tends to oppose increased emphasis on marketing as it is seen as undermining functional power bases.

2 **Slow learning** – most companies are only capable of slowly embracing the marketing concept. In the banking industry, Kotler says that marketing has passed through five stages. In the first marketing was regarded as sales promotion and publicity. Then it was taken to be smiling and providing a friendly atmosphere. Banks moved on to segmentation and innovation, and then regarded marketing as positioning. Finally, they came to see marketing as marketing analysis, planning and control.

3 **Fast forgetting** – companies which embrace marketing
   concepts tend, over time, to lose touch with core marketing principles. Various US companies have sought to
   establish their products in Europe with little knowledge
   of the differences in the marketplace.

For all the practical difficulties and the limitations of our
concept of marketing, Kotler regards it as the essence of
business and more. 'Good companies will meet needs; great
companies will create markets,' he writes. 'Market leadership
is gained by envisioning new products, services, lifestyles, and
ways to raise living standards. There is a vast difference
between companies that offer me-too products and those that
create new product and service values not even imagined by
the marketplace. Ultimately, marketing at its best is about
value creation and raising the world's living standards.'

24

TED LEVITT

Innovation in Marketing

1962

Hamel on Levitt

"If Ted Levitt had done nothing else in his career – and he did plenty – he would have earned his keep on this planet with the article, 'Marketing myopia'. Managers get wrapped up inside their products (railroads) and lose sight of the fundamental benefits customers are seeking (transportation). Equally provocative was Ted's 1983 *Harvard Business Review* article, 'The globalization of markets'. While some argue that markets will never become truly global, there are few companies that are betting against the general trend.**"**

Ted Levitt

Born in Germany in 1925, **Ted Levitt** is the leading marketing guru of the last thirty years. He is a Professor at Harvard Business School and former editor of the *Harvard Business Review*.

Levitt is the author of *The Marketing Mode* (1969), *The Marketing Imagination* (1983) and *Thinking About Management* (1991). His recent work has charted the emergence of global brands.

T ed Levitt's fame was secured early in his career with 'Marketing myopia' (Levitt, 1960), a *Harvard Business Review* article which enjoyed unprecedented success and attention, selling over 500,000 reprints. It has since been reproduced in virtually every collection of key marketing texts – and by Levitt in his 1962 book *Innovation in Marketing*.

In 'Marketing myopia' Levitt argues that the central preoccupation of corporations should be with satisfying customers rather than simply producing goods. Companies should be marketing-led rather than production-led and the lead must come from the chief executive and senior management – 'Management must think of itself not as producing products but as providing customer-creating value satisfactions.' (In his ability to coin new management jargon, as well as his thinking, Levitt was ahead of his time.) 'Marketing myopia' is, as Levitt later admitted, a manifesto rather than a deeply academic article. It embraces ideas which had already been explored by others – Levitt acknowledges, for example, his debt to Peter Drucker's *The Practice of Management*.

At the time of Levitt's article, the fact that companies were production-led is not open to question. Henry Ford's success in mass production had fueled the belief that low-cost production was the key to business success. Ford persisted in his belief that he knew what customers wanted, long after they had decided otherwise. (Even so, Levitt salutes Ford's marketing prowess arguing that the mass production techniques he used were a means to a marketing end rather than an end in themselves.)

Levitt observes that production-led thinking inevitably leads to narrow perspectives. He argues that companies must broaden their view of the nature of their business. Otherwise their customers will soon be forgotten. 'The railroads are in trouble today not because the need was filled by others ... but because it was not filled by the railroads themselves,' writes Levitt. 'They let others take customers away from them because they assumed themselves to be in the railroad business rather than in the transportation business. The reason they defined their industry wrong was because they were railroad-oriented instead of transportation-oriented; they were product-oriented instead of customer-oriented.' The railroad business was constrained, in Levitt's view, by a lack of willingness to expand its horizons.

Levitt goes on to level similar criticisms at other industries The film industry failed to respond to the growth of television because it regarded itself as being in the business of making movies rather than providing entertainment. (Interestingly, this can be applied to the resurgence of Disney in recent years – once the company began to regard itself as a provider of family entertainment in a variety of formats, rather than a children's film maker, it became spectacularly successful.)

Growth, writes Levitt, can never be taken for granted – 'In truth, there is no such thing as a growth industry'. Growth is not a matter of being in a particular industry, but in being perceptive enough to spot where future growth may lie. History, says Levitt, is filled with companies which fall into 'undetected decay' usually for a number of reasons. First, they assume that the growth in their particular market will continue so long as the population grows in size and wealth. Second is the belief that a product cannot be surpassed. Third, there is a tendency to place faith in the ability of improved production techniques to deliver lower costs and, therefore, higher profits. 'Mass production industries are impelled by a great drive to produce all they can. The prospect of steeply declining unit costs as output rises is more than most companies can usually resist. The profit possibilities look spectacular. All effort focuses on production. The result is that marketing gets neglected,' Levitt writes. Finally, there is concentration on the product as this lends itself to measurement and analysis.

These insights have proved themselves depressingly

accurate. Indeed, many of today's leading thinkers, such as Pascale and Peters, continually re-emphasize Levitt's message that there is no such thing as a growth industry. Success breeds complacency and complacency leads to failure. This is a fact of business life as true in the late 1990s as it was in the early 1960s.

In 'Marketing myopia' Levitt also makes a telling distinction between the tasks of selling and marketing. 'Selling concerns itself with the tricks and techniques of getting people to exchange their cash for your product. It is not concerned with the values that the exchange is all about. And it does not, as marketing invariably does, view the entire business process as consisting of a tightly integrated effort to discover, create, arouse, and satisfy customer needs,' he writes. This was picked up again in the 1980s when marketing underwent a resurgence and companies began to heed Levitt's view that they were overly oriented towards production.

Levitt's article and his subsequent work, pushed marketing to center stage. Indeed, in some cases it led to what Levitt labeled 'marketing mania' with companies 'obsessively responsive to every fleeting whim of the customer'. The main thrust of the article has stood the test of time ('I'd do it again and in the same way,' commented Levitt in 1975).

Levitt's analysis of the problem was clearly accurate – companies were production-led – though his prognosis for potential solutions was less so. If the railroads had decided they were in the transportation business it is unlikely they would have succeeded, but if they had looked at the needs and aspirations of their customers they may well have stemmed the tide.

25

NICOLO MACHIAVELLI

The Prince

1513

Hamel on Machiavelli

"We occasionally need reminding that leadership and strategy are not twentieth century inventions. It's just that in previous centuries they are more often the concerns of princes than industrialists. Yet power is a constant in human affairs, and a central theme of Machiavelli's *The Prince*. It is currently out of fashion to talk about power. We are constantly reminded that in the knowledge economy, capital wears shoes and goes home every night. No place here for the blunt instrument of power politics. But would Sumner Redstone, Bill Gates or Rupert Murdoch agree? What is interesting is that after 500 years, Machiavelli is still in print. What modern volume on leadership will be gracing bookstores in the year 2500? Does Machiavelli's longevity tell us anything about what are the deep, enduring truths of management?**"**

Nicolo Machiavelli
(1469–1527)

Nicolo Machiavelli served as an official in the Florentine government. During 14 years as Secretary of the Second Chancery, he became known as the 'Florentine secretary' and served on nearly 30 foreign missions. His work brought him into contact with some of Europe's most influential ministers and government representatives. His chief diplomatic triumph occurred when Florence obtained the surrender of Pisa.

Machiavelli's career came to an end in 1512 when the Medicis returned to power. He was then exiled from the city and later accused of being involved in a plot against the government. For this he was imprisoned and tortured on the rack. He then retired to a farm outside Florence and began a successful writing career, with books on politics as well as plays and a history of Florence.

T he late twentieth century has more than its fair share of self-improvement books. Publications promising the secrets of time management, stunning presentations and interviews fill countless bookshelves. Nearly 500 years ago, the first publication of its type was produced. Nicolo Machiavelli's *The Prince* is the sixteenth-century equivalent of Dale Carnegie's *How to Win Friends and Influence People*. Embedded beneath details of Alexander VI's tribulations lie a ready supply of aphorisms and insights which are, perhaps sadly, as appropriate to many of today's managers and organizations as they were half a millennium ago. (Indeed, Antony Jay's 1970 book, *Management and Machiavelli* developed the comparisons.)

'Like the leaders Machiavelli sought to defend, some executives tend to see themselves as the natural rulers in whose hands organizations can be safely entrusted,' says psychologist Robert Sharrock of consultants YSC. 'Theories abound on their motivation. Is it a defensive reaction against failure or a need for predictability through complete control? The effect of the power-driven Machiavellian manager is usually plain to see.'

'It is unnecessary for a prince to have all the good qualities I have enumerated, but it is very necessary to appear to have them,' Machiavelli advises, adding the suggestion that it is useful 'to be a great pretender and dissembler'. But *The Prince* goes beyond such helpful presentational hints. Like all great books, it offers something for everyone. Take Machiavelli on managing change: 'There is nothing more difficult to take in hand, more perilous to conduct, or more uncertain in its success, than to take the lead in the introduction of a new order of things.' Or on sustaining motivation: 'He ought above all things to keep his men well-organized and drilled, to follow incessantly the chase.'

Machiavelli even has advice for executives acquiring companies in other countries: 'But when states are acquired in a country differing in language, customs, or laws, there are difficulties, and good fortune and great energy are needed to hold them, and one of the greatest and most real helps would be that he who has acquired them should go and reside there... Because if one is on the spot, disorders are seen as they spring up, and one can quickly remedy them; but if one is not at hand, they are heard of only when they are great, and then one can no longer remedy them.' Executives throughout the world will be able to identify with Machiavelli's analysis.

Machiavelli is at his best in discussing leadership. Success, he says, is not down to luck or genius, but 'happy shrewdness'. In Machiavelli's hands, this is a euphemism. Elsewhere, he advises 'a Prince ought to have no other aim or thought, nor select anything else for his study, than war and its rules and discipline; for this is the sole art that belongs to him who rules'.

The Prince also examines the perils facing the self-made leader when they reach the dizzy heights: 'Those who solely by good fortune become princes from being private citizens have little trouble in rising, but much in keeping atop; they have not any difficulties on the way up, because they fly, but they have many when they reach the summit.'

Above all, Machiavelli is the champion of leadership through cunning and intrigue, the triumph of force over reason. An admirer of Borgia, Machiavelli had a dismal view of human nature. Unfortunately, as he sagely points out, history has repeatedly proved that a combination of being armed to the teeth and devious is more likely to allow you to achieve your objectives. It is all very well being good, says Machiavelli, but the leader 'should know how to enter into evil when necessity commands'.

26

DOUGLAS McGREGOR

The Human Side of Enterprise

1960

Hamel on McGregor

"Over the last forty years we have been slowly abandoning a view of human beings as nothing more than warm-blooded cogs in the industrial machine. People can be trusted; people want to do the right thing; people are capable of imagination and ingenuity – these were McGregor's fundamental premises, and they underlie the work of modern management thinkers from Drucker to Deming to Peters, and the employment practices of the world's most progressive and successful companies."

Douglas McGregor (1906–64)

Trained at the City College of Detroit and at Harvard, **Douglas McGregor** was a social psychologist who spent his career as President of Antioch College (1948–1954) and as a Professor of Management at MIT. Despite a limited number of publications and his short life, McGregor's work remains highly significant. He was a central figure in the Human Relations School which emerged at the end of the 1950s (and which included Maslow and Herzberg among its other luminaries).

'McGregor was a role model, and in many ways I emulated his career,' says Warren Bennis. 'McGregor had a gift of getting toward the zone of understanding that would truly affect practitioners. Doug was not a great scholar, but he had that quality of unbridled lucidity for taking what was then referred to as behavioral science research and deploying it in a way that it really would have resonance for practitioners.'

I n the preface to *The Human Side of Enterprise* Douglas McGregor writes: 'This volume is an attempt to substantiate the thesis that the human side of enterprise is "all of a piece" – that the theoretical assumptions management holds about controlling its human resources determine the whole character of the enterprise.'

The Human Side of Enterprise remains a classic text of its time and of the Human Relations school. McGregor's study of work and motivation fitted in with the concerns of the middle and late 1960s when the large monolithic corporation was at its most dominant, and the world at its most questioning. The book sold 30,000 copies in its peak year of 1965, at that time an unprecedented figure.

In *The Human Side of Enterprise*, McGregor presents two ways of describing managers' thinking: Theory X and Theory Y.

Theory X is traditional carrot and stick thinking built on 'the assumption of the mediocrity of the masses'. This assumes that workers are inherently lazy, need to be supervised and motivated, and regard work as a necessary evil to provide money. The premises of Theory X, writes McGregor, are '(1) that the average human has an inherent dislike of work and will avoid it if he can, (2) that people, therefore, need to be coerced, controlled, directed, and threatened with punishment to get them to put forward adequate effort toward the organization's ends and (3) that the typical human prefers to be directed, wants to avoid responsibility, has relatively little ambition, and wants security above all'.

McGregor lamented that Theory X 'materially influences managerial strategy in a wide sector of American industry,' and observed 'if there is a single assumption that pervades conventional organizational theory it is that authority is the central, indispensable means of managerial control'.

'The human side of enterprise today is fashioned from propositions and beliefs such as these,' writes McGregor, before going on to conclude that 'this behavior is not a consequence of man's inherent nature. It is a consequence rather of the nature of industrial organizations, of management philosophy, policy, and practice.' It is not people who have made organizations, but organizations which have transformed the perspectives, aspirations and behavior of people.

The other extreme is described by McGregor as Theory Y which is based on the principle that people want and need to work. If this is the case, then organizations need to develop the individual's commitment to its objectives, and then to liberate his or her abilities on behalf of those objectives. McGregor described the assumptions behind Theory Y: '(1) that the expenditure of physical and mental effort in work is as natural as in play or rest – the typical human doesn't inherently dislike work; (2) external control and threat of punishment are not the only means for bringing about effort toward a company's ends; (3) commitment to objectives is a function of the rewards associated with their achievement – the most important of such rewards is the satisfaction of ego and can be the direct product of effort directed toward an organization's purposes; (4) the average human being learns, under the right conditions, not only to accept but to seek responsibility; and (5) the capacity to exercise a relatively high degree of imagination, ingenuity, and creativity in the solution of organizational problems is widely, not narrowly, distributed in the population.'

Theories X and Y are not simplistic stereotypes. McGregor is realistic: 'It is no more possible to create an organization today which will be a full, effective application of this theory than it was to build an atomic power plant in 1945. There are many formidable obstacles to overcome.'

The Human Side of Enterprise also explores a number of other areas. For example, McGregor examines the process of acquiring new skills and identifies four kinds of learning relevant for managers: intellectual knowledge; manual skills; problem-solving skills; social interaction. The last element is, says McGregor, outside the confines of normal teaching and learning methods. 'We normally get little feedback of real value concerning the impact of our behavior on others. If they don't behave as we desire, it is easy to blame their stupidity, their adjustment, their peculiarities. Above all, it isn't considered good taste to give this kind of feedback in most social settings. Instead, it is discussed by our colleagues when we are not present to learn about it.' McGregor recommends the use of T-groups, then in their early stages, in which group participation was used to help people extend their insights into their own and other people's behavior.

The common complaint against McGregor's Theories X and Y is that they are mutually exclusive, two incompatible ends of an endless spectrum. To counter this, before he died in 1964, McGregor was developing Theory Z, a theory which synthesized the organizational and personal imperatives. The concept of Theory Z was later seized upon by William Ouchi. In his book of the same name, he analyzed Japanese working methods. Here, he found fertile ground for many of the ideas McGregor was proposing for Theory Z – lifetime employment, concern for employees including their social life, informal control, decisions made by consensus, slow promotion, excellent transmittal of information from top to bottom and bottom to top with the help of middle management, commitment to the firm and high concern for quality.

In another development from McGregor's original argument, John Morse and Jay Lorsch(1970) argued that 'the appropriate pattern of organization is contingent on the nature of the work to be done and the particular needs of the people involved'. They labeled their approach 'contingency theory', a pragmatic juxtaposition of Theories X and Y.

It is worth noting that Theory Y was more than mere theorizing. In the early 1950s, McGregor helped design a Proctor & Gamble plant in Georgia. Built on the Theory Y model with self-managing teams its performance soon surpassed other P&G plants. This suggests that Theory Y works, though it has largely remained consigned to textbooks rather than being put into practice on the factory floor.

27

ABRAHAM MASLOW

Motivation and Personality

1954

Hamel on Maslow

"However subtle and variegated the original theory, time tends to reduce it to its most communicable essence: hence Maslow's 'hierarchy of needs', Pascale's 'seven Ss', Michael Porter's 'five forces', and the Boston Consulting Group's growth/share matrix. Yet there is no framework that has so broadly infiltrated organizational life as Maslow's hierarchy of needs. Perhaps this is because it speaks so directly to the aspirations each of us holds for ourself."

Abraham Maslow (1908–1970)

Abraham Maslow was an American behavioral psychologist. Born in Brooklyn, he trained at the University of Wisconsin. His career involved working in management and academia. As an academic, he was initially interested in the social behavior of primates and worked at Columbia University as a research fellow, Brooklyn College as an associate professor, the Western Behavioral Sciences Institute and later at Brandeis University in Massachusetts. It was while working at Brandeis that he wrote *Motivation and Personality*. His other books included *Towards a Psychology of Being* (1962); *Eupsychian Management* (1965); *The Psychology of Science* (1967) and *The Farther Reaches of Human Nature* (1971).

In two spells in industry, he worked as a plant manager at the Maslow Cooperage Corporation in Pleasanton, California, in the late 1940s and later he worked with a Southern Californian electronics company.

braham Maslow was a member of the Human Relations School of the late fifties. *Motivation and Personality* is best known for its 'hierarchy of needs' – a concept which was first published by Maslow in 1943. In this, Maslow argues that there is an ascending scale of needs which need to be understood if people are to be motivated.

First are the fundamental physiological needs of warmth, shelter and food. 'It is quite true that man lives by bread alone – when there is no bread. But what happens to man's desires when there is plenty of bread and when his belly is chronically filled?' Maslow asks.

Once basic physiological needs are met, others emerge to dominate. 'If the physiological needs are relatively well gratified, there then emerges a new set of needs, which we may categorize roughly as the safety needs,' writes Maslow. 'A man, in this state, if it is extreme enough and chronic enough, may be characterized as living almost for safety alone.'

Next on the hierarchy are social or love needs, and ego, or self-esteem, needs. Ultimately, as man moves up the scale, with each need being satisfied comes what Maslow labels 'self-actualization', the individual achieves their own personal potential. (Later, Maslow created the word 'Eupsychian' to describe 'the culture that would be generated by 1,000 self-actualizing people on some sheltered island where they would not be interfered with'.)

While the hierarchy of needs provides a rational framework for motivation, its flaw lies in the nature of humanity. Man always wants more. When asked what salary they would be comfortable with, people routinely – no matter what their income – name a figure which is around twice their current income.

Even so, Maslow's hierarchy of needs contributed to the emergence of human relations as a discipline and to a sea-change in how motivation was perceived. Instead of being simplistically regarded as driven by punishment and deprivation, motivation became intrinsically linked to rewards. Maslow's concept of 'self-actualization' is increasingly the subject of managerial texts.

28

HENRY MINTZBERG

The Nature of Managerial Work

1973

Hamel on Mintzberg

"Five reasons why I like Henry Mintzberg. He is a worldclass iconoclast. He loves the messy world of real companies (see *The Nature of Managerial Work*). He is a master storyteller. He is conceptual *and* pragmatic. He doesn't believe in easy answers."

Henry Mintzberg

Henry Mintzberg is 'perhaps the world's premier management thinker,' says Tom Peters.[1] Mintzberg is Professor of Management at McGill University, Montreal and at INSEAD in Fontainebleau, France. He has recently been overseeing a venture by five business schools in Canada, the UK, France, India and Japan to create a next-generation master's program for the development of managers. Mintzberg's original training was in mechanical engineering. He has a Ph.D. in management from MIT in Boston and honorary degrees from the Universities of Venice, Lund, Lausanne and Montreal.

His reputation has been made not by popularizing new techniques, but by rethinking the fundamentals of strategy and structure, management and planning. He takes an idiosyncratic, sometimes eccentric, but always interesting, view on virtually every aspect of managerial life. His work on strategy, in particular his ideas of 'emergent strategy' and 'grass-roots strategy making', has been highly influential.

He has won McKinsey prizes for the best article in the *Harvard Business Review* and is the author of *Mintzberg on Management: Inside our Strange World of Organizations* (1989), *Structure in Fives: Designing Effective Organizations* (1983) *The Nature of Managerial Work* (1973), and *The Rise and Fall of Strategic Planning* (1994).

hat managers actually do, how they do it and why, are fundamental questions. There are a number of generally accepted answers. Managers have a vision of themselves – which they largely persist in believing and propagating – that they sit in solitude contemplating the great strategic issues of the day; that they make time to reach the best decisions and that their meetings are high-powered, concentrating on the meta-narrative rather than the nitty-gritty.

The reality largely went unexplored until Henry Mintzberg's *The Nature of Managerial Work*. Instead of accepting pat answers to perennial questions, Mintzberg went in search of the reality. He simply observed what a number of managers actually did. The resulting book blew away the managerial mystique.

Instead of spending time contemplating the long term, Mintzberg found that managers were slaves to the moment, moving from task to task with every move dogged by another diversion, another call. The median time spent on any one issue was a mere nine minutes. In *The Nature of Managerial Work*, Mintzberg identifies the characteristics of the manager at work:

- performs a great quantity of work at an unrelenting pace
- undertakes activities marked by variety, brevity and fragmentation
- has a preference for issues which are current, specific and non-routine
- prefers verbal rather than written means of communication
- acts within a web of internal and external contacts
- is subject to heavy constraints but can exert some control over the work.'

From these observations, Mintzberg identified the manager's 'work roles' as:

- **Interpersonal roles**
  Figurehead: representing the organization/unit to outsiders
  Leader: motivating subordinates, unifying effort
  Liaiser: maintaining lateral contacts
- **Informational roles**
  Monitor: of information flows
  Disseminator: of information to subordinates
  Spokesman: transmission of information to outsiders
- **Decisional roles**
  Entrepreneur: initiator and designer of change
  Disturbance handler: handling non-routine events
  Resource allocator: deciding who gets what and who will do what
  Negotiator: negotiating.

'All managerial work encompasses these roles, but the prominence of each role varies in different managerial jobs,' writes Mintzberg.

Strangely, *The Nature of Managerial Work* has produced few worthwhile imitators. Researchers appear content to rely on neat case studies filled with retrospective wisdom and which are outdated as soon as they are written; or general interviews in which managers pontificate generally without being tied down to particulars. The actual work of managing enterprises often goes unnoticed behind the fashion and hyperbole.

Notes
1 Peters, Tom, 'Strategic planning, RIP', 25 March, 1994.

29

HENRY MINTZBERG

The Rise and Fall of Strategic Planning

1994

Hamel on Mintzberg

"Henry views strategic planning as a ritual, devoid of creativity and meaning. He is undoubtedly right when he argues that planning doesn't produce strategy. But rather than use the last chapter of the book to create a new charter for planners, Henry might have put his mind to the question of where strategies actually do come from!"

enry Mintzberg's *The Rise and Fall of Strategic Planning* reflects a general dissatisfaction with the process of strategic planning – research by the US Planning Forum found that only 25 percent of companies considered their planning processes to be effective and OC&C Strategy Consultants observed in a pamphlet that 'the humane thing to do with most strategic planning processes is to kill them off'.

Mintzberg has long been a critic of formulae and analysis-driven strategic planning. In *The Rise and Fall of Strategic Planning*, he remorselessly destroys much conventional wisdom and proposes his own interpretations.

He defines planning as 'a formalized system for codifying, elaborating and operationalizing the strategies which companies already have'. In contrast, strategy is either an 'emergent' pattern or a deliberate 'perspective'. Mintzberg argues that strategy cannot be planned. While planning is concerned with analysis, strategy making is concerned with synthesis. Today's planners are not redundant but are only valuable as strategy finders, analysts and catalysts. They are supporters of line managers, forever questioning rather than providing automatic answers. Their most effective role is in unearthing 'fledgling strategies in unexpected pockets of the organization so that consideration can be given to (expanding) them'.

Mintzberg identifies three central pitfalls to today's strategy planning practices.

First, the assumption that discontinuities can be predicated. Forecasting techniques are limited by the fact that they tend to assume that the future will resemble the past. This gives artificial reassurance and creates strategies which are liable to disintegrate as they are overtaken by events.

He points out that our passion for planning mostly flourishes during stable times such as in the 1960s. Confronted by a new world order, planners are left seeking to recreate a long-forgotten past.

Second, that planners are detached from the reality of the organization. Mintzberg is critical of the 'assumption of detachment'. 'If the system does the thinking,' he writes, 'the thought must be detached from the action, strategy from operations, (and) ostensible thinkers from doers... It is this disassociation of thinking from acting that lies close to the root of (strategic planning's) problem.'

Planners have traditionally been obsessed with gathering hard data on their industry, markets and competitors. Soft data – networks of contacts, talking with customers, suppliers and employees, using intuition and using the grapevine – have all but been ignored.

Mintzberg points out that much of what is considered 'hard' data is often anything but. There is a 'soft underbelly of hard data', typified by the fallacy of 'measuring what's measurable'. The results are limiting, for example a pronounced tendency 'to favor cost leadership strategies (emphasizing operating efficiencies, which are generally measurable) over product-leadership strategies (emphasizing innovative design or high quality, which tends to be less measurable)'.

To gain real and useful understanding of an organization's competitive situation soft data needs to be dynamically integrated into the planning process. 'Strategy-making is an immensely complex process involving the most sophisticated, subtle and at times subconscious of human cognitive and social processes,' writes Mintzberg. 'While hard data may inform the intellect, it is largely soft data that generate wisdom. They may be difficult to "analyze", but they are indispensable for synthesis – the key to strategy making.'

The third and final flaw identified by Mintzberg is the assumption that strategy-making can be formalized. The left-side of the brain has dominated strategy formulation with its emphasis on logic and analysis. Overly structured, this creates a narrow range of options. Alternatives which do not fit into the pre-determined structure are ignored. The right-side of the brain needs to become part of the process with its emphasis on intuition and creativity. 'Planning by its very nature,' concludes Mintzberg, 'defines and preserves categories. Creativity, by its very nature, creates categories or rearranges established ones. This is why strategic planning can neither provide creativity, nor deal with it when it emerges by other means.' Mold-breaking strategies 'grow initially like weeds, they are not cultivated like tomatoes in a hothouse... (They) can take root in all kinds of places'.

Strategy-making, as presented by Mintzberg is:

- derived from synthesis
- informal and visionary, rather than programmed and formalized
- reliant on divergent thinking, intuition and using the subconscious. This leads to outbursts of creativity as new discoveries are made
- irregular, unexpected, *ad hoc*, instinctive. It upsets stable patterns
- is based on managers being adaptive information manipulators, opportunists, rather than aloof conductors
- done in times of instability characterized by discontinuous change
- the result of an approach which takes in broad perspectives and is, therefore, visionary, and involves a variety of actors capable of experimenting and then integrating.

The Rise and Fall of Strategic Planning attracted a great deal of attention and some vituperative debate. 'In many ways, the book's title should be reversed to the fall and rise of planning,' observed Christopher Lorenz in the *Financial Times*, arguing that the book represented the 'mellowing of Mintzberg'.

Mintzberg's work brought a spirited response from the defenders of strategy. Andrew Campbell, co-author of

Corporate-Level Strategy, wrote: 'Strategic planning is not futile. Research has shown that some companies – both conglomerates and more focused groups – have strategic planning processes that add real value.' The solution, according to Campbell (1994) is not to deem planning an inappropriate corporate activity but will only occur when 'the corporate center develops a value-creating, corporate-level strategy and builds the management processes needed to implement it'.

The debate rumbles on though many would regard *The Rise and Fall of Strategic Planning* as a quantum leap forward in strategic thinking.

30

KENICHI OHMAE

The Mind of the Strategist

1982

Hamel on Ohmae

"I loved this book! At a time when most strategy savants were focused either on the process of planning (Ansoff and his followers) or on the determinants of successful, i.e. profitable, strategies (Michael Porter), Kenichi Ohmae challenged managers to think in new ways. Strategy doesn't come from a calendar-driven process; it isn't the product of a systematic search for ways of earning above average profits; strategy comes from viewing the world in new ways. Strategy starts with an ability to think in new and unconventional ways. Henry, Kenichi has something to tell you!**"**

Kenichi Ohmae

Kenichi Ohmae (born 1943) is a Japanese who was first Americanized (Kenichi became Ken to his US colleagues) and then globalized. Ohmae is enormously gifted. A concert-standard flautist, he is also a nuclear physicist, prodigious author with dozens of books to his credit, politician and long-time star of the consulting firm, McKinsey and Company. Indeed, when he left McKinsey to stand for the governorship of Tokyo in 1995, the consultancy firm's departure announcement noted Ohmae was 'a great consultant, a compelling speaker, an incredibly prolific writer, a musician and a motorcyclist'. The significance of the latter accomplishment is difficult to determine.

Ohmae is a graduate of Waseda University, the Tokyo Institute of Technology, and has a Ph.D. in nuclear engineering from Massachusetts Institute of Technology. He joined McKinsey in 1972, becoming managing director of its Tokyo office. He has been an adviser to the former Japanese Prime Minister Nakasone.

The Financial Times described him as 'a personality in a land where outspoken personalities are rare. And while most Japanese are anxious not to offend, Ohmae is blunt and often downright rude ... he is Japan's only successful management guru.'

His best known books, in the West at least, include *Japan Business: Obstacles and Opportunities* (1983), *Triad Power: The Coming Shape of Global Competition* (1985), *Beyond National Borders* (1987) and *The End of the Nation State* (1995).

he Mind of the Strategist by Kenichi Ohmae was published in Japan in 1975, but did not reach the American market until 1982. 'The author's sometimes imperfect English combines with a simple, personal style to give this book a great deal of charm,' observed the *Harvard Business Review* in patronizing mood.

The subtitle in the first edition was 'The art of Japanese business' and the book was published in the West at the height of enthusiasm and interest in Japanese management methods – when the book was first published in Japan, the West remained studiously uninterested in the possibility of learning from Japanese best practice.

In *The Mind of the Strategist* Ohmae challenges the simplistic, but then widely held belief, that Japanese management was a matter of company songs and lifetime employment. Instead, Ohmae argues that Japanese success could be significantly attributed to the nature of Japanese strategic thinking. This, says Ohmae, is 'basically creative and intuitive and rational' – though none of these characteristics were evident in the usual Western stereotype of Japanese management. Offering solace to the bemused and increasingly uncompetitive West, Ohmae suggests that the necessary creativity can be learnt.

Ohmae points out that unlike large US corporations, Japanese businesses tend not to have large strategic planning staffs. Instead they often have a single, naturally talented strategist with 'an idiosyncratic mode of thinking in which company, customers, and competition merge in a dynamic interaction out of which a comprehensive set of objectives and plans for action eventually crystallizes'.

Another area of fundamental difference explored by Ohmae is the role of the customer who is at the heart of the Japanese approach to strategy and key to corporate values. At the time customers were generally noticeable by their absence from Western strategic planning and corporate values. 'In the construction of any business strategy, three main players must be taken into account: the corporation itself, the customer, and the competition. Each of these "strategic three Cs" is a living entity with its own interests and objectives. We shall call them, collectively, the "strategic triangle",' says Ohmae. 'Seen in the context of the strategic triangle, the job of the strategist is to achieve superior performance, relative to competition, in the key factors for success of the business. At the same time, the strategist must be sure that his strategy properly matches the strengths of the corporation with the needs of a clearly defined market. Positive matching of the needs and objectives of the two parties involved is required for a lasting good relationship; without it, the corporation's long-term viability may be at stake.'

The central thrust of the book is that strategy as epitomized by the Japanese approach is irrational and nonlinear. (Previously, the Japanese had been feted in the West for the brilliance of their rationality and the far-sighted remorselessness of their thinking.) 'In strategic thinking, one first seeks a clear understanding of the particular character of each element of a situation and then makes the fullest possible use of human brain power to restructure the elements in the most advantageous way,' writes Ohmae.

'Phenomena and events in the real world do not always fit a linear model. Hence the most reliable means of dissecting a situation into its constituent parts and reassembling them in the desired pattern is not a step-by-step methodology such as systems analysis. Rather, it is that ultimate non-linear thinking tool, the human brain. True strategic thinking thus contrasts sharply with the conventional mechanical systems approach based on linear thinking. But it also contrasts with the approach that stakes everything on intuition, reaching conclusions without any real breakdown or analysis.'

The Mind of the Strategist is not an unquestioning eulogy to the Japanese approach to strategy. Indeed, Ohmae notes the decline in naturally strategic thinkers in both Japan and the West. Both systems, he says, encourage orthodoxy to the extent that innovative strategic thinking is neither encouraged nor possible.

An effective business strategy, Ohmae says, 'is one, by which a company can gain significant ground on its competitors at an acceptable costs to itself'. There are four main ways of achieving this – 'In each of these four methods, the principal concern is to avoid doing the same thing, on the same battle-ground, as the competition,' Ohmae explains.

The first method is through focusing on the key factors for success (KFSs). Certain functional or operating areas within every business are more critical for success in that particular business environment than others. If you concentrate effort into these areas and your competitors do not, this is a source of competitive advantage. The problem, of course, is identifying what these key factors for success are. 'The most effective shortcut to major success seems to be to jump quickly to the top of the rank by concentrating major resources early on a single strategically significant function,' says Ohmae. 'All of today's industry leaders, without exception, began by bold deployment of strategies based on KFS.'

The second route is by building on relative superiority. When all competitors are seeking to compete on the KFSs, a company can exploit any differences in competitive conditions. For example, it can make use of technology or sales networks not in direct competition with its rivals.

The third method is through pursuing aggressive initiatives. Frequently, the only way to win against a much larger, entrenched competitor is to upset the competitive environment, by undermining the value of its KFSs – changing the rules of the game by introducing new KFSs.

The final route to an effective strategy is through utilizing strategic degrees of freedom. By this, Ohmae means that the company can focus upon innovation in areas which are 'untouched by competitors'.

The Mind of the Strategist began the process of questioning the then pervasive Japanese mythology through providing interpretations of strategy which were not hidebound by habitual cultural or traditional behavior. In his subsequent works, Ohmae's perspectives have broadened and he develops the highly original ideas of *The Mind of the Strategist* still further.

31

KENICHI OHMAE

The Borderless World

1990

Hamel on Ohmae

"So the world is becoming interdependent.
Hardly news to companies like Dow Chemical,
IBM, Ford or Nestlé. But in 1990 this was still
news to Japanese companies (and politicians)
who typically defined 'globalization' as big open
export markets, and maybe a factory in Ten-
nessee. Kenichi challenged Japanese companies,
and myopic executives elsewhere, to develop a
more sophisticated view of what it means to be
global. Just what balance will ultimately be
struck between the forces of globalization and
the forces of nationalism and tribalism remains
to be seen.**"**

*T*he *Borderless World* is an ambitious book exploring 'the new logic of the global marketplace' as well as what Kenichi Ohmae calls 'power and strategy in the interlinked economy'.

To the three Cs of his previous works, Ohmae adds two more – country (rather tortuously defined as 'the various government-created environments in which global organizations must operate') and currency ('the exposure of such organizations to fluctuations in foreign exchange rates'). These two additional elements are now key to the formulation of any strategy – 'When a sudden fluctuation in trade policy or exchange rates can turn an otherwise brilliant strategy into a seemingly irreparable hemorrhage of cash, making arrangements to deal with such fluctuations must lie at the very heart of strategy'.

Ohmae now defines strategy as 'creating sustaining values for the customer far better than those of competitors. It therefore means first of all invention and the commercialization of invention. Most people in big companies have forgotten how to invent'. As a result, Ohmae argues that 'it's time for big companies to relearn the art of invention. But this time they must learn to manage invention in industries or businesses that are global, where you have to get world-scale economies and yet tailor products to key markets'.

Strategy, says Ohmae, is about more than being better than the competition. This encourages companies to become fixated with the competition so that in formulating their strategy, they are driven by the strategy of their competitors. 'Competitive realities are what you test possible strategies against; you define them in terms of customers. Tit-for-tat responses to what competitors do may be appropriate, but they are largely reactive. They come second, after your real strategy. Before you test yourself against competition, your strategy should encompass the determination to create value for customers,' states Ohmae.

To Ohmae, countries are mere governmental creations.

In the Interlinked Economy (made up of the Triad of the US, Europe and Japan) consumers are not driven to purchase things through nationalistic sentiments – no matter what politicians suggest or say. 'At the cash register, you don't care about country of origin or country of residence. You don't think about employment figures or trade deficits,' Ohmae writes. This, he argues, also applies to industrial consumers.

The Borderless World concludes with a 'Declaration of Interdependence toward the world' signed by Ohmae and McKinsey's Fred Gluck and Herbert Henzler. It is immodestly noted below that 'this statement ... is one we each embrace and believe to be the best possible course for all countries and governments to follow'.

In the declaration, the trio contend that the role of central governments must change to 'allow individuals access to the best and cheapest goods and services from anywhere in the world; help corporations provide stable and rewarding jobs anywhere in the world regardless of the corporation's national identity; coordinate activities with other governments to minimize conflicts arising from narrow interests; and avoid abrupt changes in economic and social fundamentals'. It calls on governments to 'deal collectively with traditionally parochial affairs' including taxation.

This manifesto for the future is as broad ranging as it is, in political reality, unlikely. *The Borderless World* has, however, fueled debates about the role of governments and the relationship between governments and the business world which have yet to be resolved. Ohmae has since gone on to explore the role of nations still further and now suggests that we have reached a time when 'the end of the nation state' is imminent.

32

C. NORTHCOTE PARKINSON

Parkinson's Law

1958

Hamel on Parkinson

"Yes, I know that bureaucracy is dead. We're not managers any more, we're leaders. We're not slaves to our work, we've been liberated. And all those layers of paper-shuffling administrators between the CEO and the order-takers, they're all gone, right? Well then, why does a re-reading of *Parkinson's Law*, written in 1958, at the apex of corporate bureaucracy, still ring true? *Parkinson's Law* was to the fifties what *The Dilbert Principle* is to the 1990s. (What, Scott Adams isn't in here?)**"**

C. Northcote Parkinson
(1909–1993)

C. Northcote Parkinson studied history at Cambridge and then undertook a Ph.D. at King's College London. He subsequently held a variety of academic posts in the UK and the US, and later in his career was Raffles Professor of History at the University of Malaya. His theories on the machinations of administrative life were developed during five years of army service during World War Two.

Parkinson's sequel to *Parkinson's Law* was *The Law and the Profits* (1960) which introduces Parkinson's Second Law: expenditure rises to meet income.

arkinson's Law is an amusing interlude in management literature. It was written by C. Northcote Parkinson in the late 1950s when the Human Relations School in the United States was beginning to flower and thinkers were actively questioning the bureaucracy which had grown up alongside mass production. Max Weber's model of a paper-producing bureaucratic machine appeared to have been brought to fruition as the arteries of major organizations became clogged with layer upon layer of managerial administrators.

Parkinson's Law is simply that work expands to fill the time available for its completion. As a result, companies grow without thinking of how much they are producing. Even if growth in numbers fails to make them more money, companies grow and people become busier and busier. Parkinson observes that 'an official wants to multiply subordinates, not rivals' and 'officials make work for each other'.

If only Frederick Taylor had met Parkinson, the history of managerial thinking may have been dramatically altered. Parkinson wryly and accurately debunks the notion of a particular task having an optimum time for completion. There are no rules – it depends on the person doing the job and their unique situation. 'An elderly lady of leisure can spend an entire day in writing and dispatching a postcard to her niece at Bognor Regis,' writes Parkinson. 'An hour will be spent in finding the postcard, another in hunting for spectacles, half-an-hour in a search for the address, an hour and a quarter in composition, and twenty minutes in deciding whether or not to take an umbrella when going to the pillar-box in the next street. The total effort which would occupy a busy man for three minutes all told, may, in this fashion, leave another person prostrate after a day of doubt, anxiety and toil.'

Parkinson is at his best when describing the life of the humble administrator. Faced with the decreasing energy of age and a feeling of being overworked, he observes that administrators face three options: resign, halve the work with a colleague or ask for two more subordinates. 'There is probably no instance in civil service history of choosing any but the third alternative,' Parkinson reflects.

The theory is not simply an exercise in superficial cynicism. Parkinson backs it up with statistics. He points out, for example, that the number of admiralty officials in the British Navy increased by 78 percent between 1914 and 1928 while the number of ships fell by 67 percent and the number of officers and men by 31 percent. Parkinson concludes that the expansion of administrators tends to take on a life of its own – 'The Officials would have multiplied at the same rate had there been no actual seamen at all.' (In the 1990s, Parkinson's Law can perhaps be applied to the preponderance of management jargon in the Navy which has increased as numbers have plummeted.)

What makes *Parkinson's Law* memorable is the sympathy Parkinson evokes for the humble administrators who know no other way. He waxes lyrical as administrator 'A' leaves work: 'The last of the office lights are being turned off in the gathering dusk which marks the end of another day's administrative toil. Among the last to leave, A reflects, with bowed shoulders and a wry smile, that late hours, like gray hairs, are among the penalties of success.'

Parkinson does not propose solutions. 'It is not the business of the botanist to eradicate the weeds. Enough for him if he can tell us just how fast they grow,' he explains. *Parkinson's Law* is a kind of Catch-22 of the business world, by turns irreverent and humorous, but with a darker underside of acute observation.

Parkinson warns of the perils of taking any book on the subject of business seriously: 'Heaven forbid that students should cease to read a book on the science of public or business administration provided that these works are classified as fiction.'

33

RICHARD PASCALE & ANTHONY ATHOS

The Art of Japanese Management

1981

Hamel on Pascale & Athos

"Japan phobia has subsided a bit, helped by a strong yen, inept Japanese macroeconomic policy, and the substantial efforts of many Western companies to rebuild their competitiveness. While Pascale and Athos undoubtedly overstated the unique capabilities of Japanese management (is Matsushita really that much better managed than Hewlett-Packard?), they successfully challenged the unstated assumption that America was the font of all managerial wisdom. Since *The Art of Japanese Management* hit the bookstores, American companies have learned much from Japan. Pascale and Athos deserve credit for setting the learning agenda."

Richard Pascale & Anthony Athos

Richard Pascale was a member of the faculty of Stanford's Graduate School of Business for 20 years and taught the most popular course in its MBA program – a course on organizational survival. Born in 1938, he is now a leading business consultant. He is also the author of *Managing on the Edge* (1990). He has been a White House Fellow, Special Assistant to the Secretary of Labor and Senior Staff of a White House Task Force reorganizing the President's executive office.

Anthony Athos was a member of the Harvard Business School faculty for many years.

he Art of Japanese Management, which Richard Pascale co-authored with Harvard's Anthony Athos, was one of the first business bestsellers. It played a crucial role in the discovery of Japanese management techniques as Pascale and Athos considered how a country the same size as Montana could be outstripping the American industrial juggernaut. 'In 1980, Japan's GNP was third highest in the world and, if we extrapolate current trends, it would be number one by the year 2000,' warn Pascale and Athos.

The roots of the book lie in Pascale's work with the US National Commission on Productivity. Having initially thought that lessons from Japan were limited for cultural reasons, Pascale decided more fertile ground lay in looking at Japanese companies in the US. The research for the book eventually covered 34 companies over six years.

For the American readership, *The Art of Japanese Management* provides harsh home truths. 'If anything, the extent of Japanese superiority over the United States in industrial competitiveness is underestimated,' say Pascale and Athos, observing that 'a major reason for the superiority of the Japanese is their managerial skill'. In its comparisons of US and Japanese companies, *The Art of Japanese Management* provides rare insights into the truth behind the mythology of Japanese management and the inadequacy of much Western practice.

Among the key components of Japanese management identified by Pascale and Athos is that of vision, something they found to be notably lacking in the West. 'Our problem today is that the tools are there but our "vision" is limited. A great many American managers are influenced by beliefs, assumptions, and perceptions about management that unduly constrain them,' write Pascale and Athos. The book, they say, is 'not an assault on the existing tools of management, but upon the Western vision of management which circumscribes our effectiveness'.

Pascale and Athos's championing of vision proved highly

influential. Pascale now attributes much of this to his co-author: 'It was Athos who really started the entire visioning industry in the US. Back in the seventies no one had really thought about it.' Soon after *The Art of Japanese Management* a flurry of books appeared highlighting so-called visionaries. Today, corporate visions are a fact of life though many fail to match the Japanese practice mapped out by Pascale and Athos in which visions are dynamic, vivifying *modus operandi* rather than pallid or generic statements of corporate intent.

The Art of Japanese Management is, however, best known for its central concept: the Seven S framework. This emerged from a series of meetings during June 1978 between Pascale, Athos and the authors of *In Search of Excellence*, Tom Peters and Robert Waterman who were already involved in their research into excellent companies. The story of the evolution of the framework is given in *The Art of Japanese Management*.

Initially a meeting was arranged between the quartet. 'Athos said we needed an agenda for the five days otherwise we'd be driven round the bend by Peters – he's so energetic, such a scatter shot. Otherwise we wouldn't survive the five days,' Pascale now recalls. 'Athos said he had given it some thought and said there was a guy at Harvard, Chuck Gibson, who had a scheme – strategy, structure and systems. He had developed these three Ss for Harvard's PMD Program which he and Tony were in charge of. So why didn't we start with strategy on Monday then move on to structure on Tuesday and systems on Wednesday. Athos said he had a couple of his own to add – superordinate goals and shared values. I was working on *The Art of Japanese Management* so was interested in the idea of shared values. Athos insisted on superordinate goals and I contributed style. So we walked in with five of the Seven Ss.'[1]

Athos and Pascale persuaded Waterman and Peters to use alliteration. Peters and Pascale then suggested another variable was needed, one concerned with timing and implementation. Athos and Pascale proposed calling it 'sequencing'.

Julian Phillips of McKinsey who also joined the group, argued vigorously for replacing 'sequencing' with 'staff'. 'Since everyone was having trouble with sequencing it was easy to drop,' say Athos and Pascale. 'And since Peters was proposing that "people" and "power" needed somehow to be included (Athos was adding "aggregates of people" at Harvard), it was also possible to agree that staff was an addition which resolved various concerns, Thus, the final Seven S Framework came into being.'

The Seven Ss (strategy, structure, skills, staff, shared values, systems and style) are a kind of *aide memoire*, a useful memory jogger of what concerns organizations. The Seven S framework gained a great deal of attention though, as a generic statement of the issues facing organizations, it is unremarkable. (Tom Peters himself initially thought it 'corny' – though Peters and Waterman used it a year later in *In Search of Excellence*.) 'The framework is nothing more than seven important categories that managers pay attention to,' Pascale later noted in *Managing on the Edge*. 'There is nothing sacred about the number seven. There could be six or eight Ss. the value of a framework such as the Seven Ss is that it imposes an interesting discipline on the researcher.'

The Seven Ss presents a way into comparisons between US and Japanese management. Pascale and Athos conclude that the Japanese succeeded largely because of the attention they gave to the soft Ss – style, shared values, skills and staff. In contrast, the West remained preoccupied with the hard Ss of strategy, structure and systems.

Since *The Art of Japanese Management* the general trend of Western managerial thinking has been directed towards the soft Ss. Whether this has led to the West correcting the imbalance identified by Pascale and Athos is a matter of continuing debate.

Notes
1 Interview with Stuart Crainer, 23 July 1996.

34

RICHARD PASCALE

Managing on the Edge

1990

Hamel on Pascale

"In *Managing on the Edge*, Richard Pascale provides a number of useful observations on the sources of corporate vitality. One of the things I've always admired about Richard Pascale is that he focuses not on tools and techniques, but on principles and paradigms. While management bookshelves groan with the weight of simplistic how-to-books (e.g. *The One Minute Manager*), Pascale challenges managers to think, and to think deeply. Pascale forces managers to deconstruct the normative models on which they base their beliefs and actions. Seldom do business authors force us to confront so directly our managerial orthodoxies."

R ichard Pascale's *Managing on the Edge* begins with the line 'Nothing fails like success'. 'Great strengths are inevitably the root of weakness,' writes Pascale, pausing only to point out that from the *Fortune 500* of 1985, 143 had departed five years later.

Managing on the Edge presents a formidably researched and argued challenge to complacency and timidity. 'American managerial history is largely inward-focused and self-congratulatory,' writes Pascale, echoing his criticisms first aired in *The Art of Japanese Management* nine years previously.

Change, says Pascale, is a fact of business life. The trouble is we are ill-equipped to deal with it and our traditional approach to managing change is no longer applicable. 'The incremental approach to change is effective when what you want is more of what you've already got. Historically, that has been sufficient because our advantages of plentiful resources, geographical isolation, and absence of serious global competition defined a league in which we competed with ourselves and everyone played by the same rules.'

Pascale bids farewell to easy options. He is vehement in his criticism of Peters and Waterman's *In Search of Excellence*: 'Simply identifying attributes of success is like identifying attributes of people in excellent health during the age of the bubonic plague.' And argues that 'passions and obsession frequently degenerate into simplistic formulae e.g. acronyms such as KISS (Keep it simple, stupid). This book advocates wisdom and coolness at a higher level of complexity.'

Best known is Pascale's chart of the profusion of management fads. He calculates that there have been more than two dozen since the 1950s – and, of these, a dozen emerged in the five years prior to 1990.

Going on to further examine the malaise he identifies in management, Pascale contends that four factors 'drive stagnation and renewal in organizations':

1 Fit – pertains to an organization's internal consistency (unity)
2 Split – describes a variety of techniques for breaking a bigger organization into smaller units and providing them with a stronger sense of ownership and identity (plurality)
3 Contend – refers to a management process that harnesses (rather than suppresses) the contradictions that are inevitable by-products of organizations (duality)
4 Transcend – alerts us to the higher order of complexity that successfully managing the renewal process entails (vitality)

Pascale calls for a fundamental shift in perspective. 'Managerial behavior is predicated on the assumption that we should rationally order the behavior of those we manage. That mindset needs to be challenged,' he writes. Orderly answers are no longer appropriate. Instead, the new emphasis should be on asking questions (the book's final chapter is entitled 'The question is the answer'). 'Strategic planning, at best, is about posing questions, more than attempting to answer them,' Pascale suggests.

Pascale argues that successful organizations undergo a continual process of renewal. (Later he developed this theme, calling for 'corporate transformation'.) Central to achieving this is a willingness to ask questions constantly and to harness conflict for the corporate good through systems that encourage questioning. Companies must become 'engines of inquiry'.

The trouble is that managers are ill-equipped to deal with the contention that arises when fundamental questions are posed. If we are to succeed in managing on the edge then 'contention management is essential to orchestrate tensions that arise'. The book's sub-title is 'How the smartest companies use conflict to stay ahead' and Pascale estimates that 50 percent of the time when contention arises it is smoothed over and avoided. 'The forces that we have historically regarded as locked in opposition can be viewed (through a different mindset, or paradigm) as apparent opposites generating inquiry and adaptive responses,' writes Pascale. 'This is because each point of view represents a facet of reality, and these realities tend to challenge one another and raise questions. If we redefine the manager's job as maintaining a constructive level of debate, we are, in effect, holding the organization in the question. This leads to identifying blind spots and working around obstacles.' Truth – personally and organizationally – lies in the openness of vigorous debate and, as Pascale writes: 'Organizations are, in the last analysis, interactions among people.'

Managing on the Edge set the tone for much of the management thinking of the decade. Its emphasis on the need for constant change has since been developed by Pascale. He now argues that the issue of managing the way we change is a competence rather than an episodic necessity. The capability to change is a core competence in its own right.

35

TOM PETERS & ROBERT WATERMAN

In Search of Excellence

1982

Hamel on Peters & Waterman

"Let us never underestimate the market for hope. *In Search of Excellence* appeared one year after *The Art of Japanese Management*, when the industrial self-confidence of the West was at its lowest ebb ever. You, too, can be great was the message – no surprise, then, that it found a mass audience. The dividing line between simple truths, and simplistic prescription is always a thin one. For the most part, Peters and Waterman avoided the facile and the tautological. Indeed, the focus on operations research, elaborate planning systems, and (supposedly) rigorous financial analysis had, in many companies, robbed management of its soul – and certainly had taken the focus off the customer. Peters and Waterman reminded managers that success often comes from doing common things uncommonly well."

Tom Peters & Robert Waterman

Tom Peters and **Robert Waterman** were McKinsey consultants when *In Search of Excellence* was being written. Peters left the company prior to publication and Waterman two years later.

Since that time, the two have taken wildly different paths. Peters (born 1942) has become a high-profile guru, traveling the world, writing books which have been described as 'charismatic shockers'. His books include *A Passion for Excellence* (with Nancy Austin, 1985), *Thriving on Chaos* (1987), *Liberation Management* (1992) and the more recent collections *The Tom Peters Seminar* (1994) and *The Pursuit of Wow!* (1994). Peters has his own Palo Alto-based company, the Tom Peters Group, but now spends the majority of his time on his Vermont farm.

Waterman (born 1936) has a far lower profile, occasionally producing thoughtful books, but preferring to spend his time painting rather than on the seminar circuit. He has a consultancy company based in California. Since *In Search of Excellence*, Waterman has written *The Renewal Factor* (1987) and *The Frontiers of Excellence* (1994).

*I*n *Search of Excellence* by Tom Peters and Robert Waterman is the most popular management book of contemporary times. Its global sales now near six million.

Analysis of why *In Search of Excellence* is such a success has filled many magazine articles throughout the world. Peter Drucker (1987) suggested that its simplicity explained its appeal: 'The strength of the Peters book is that it forces you to look at the fundamentals. The book's great weakness – which is a strength from the point of view of its success – is that it makes managing sound so incredibly easy. All you have to do is put that book under your pillow, and it'll get done.'

Looking back, Tom Peters has an understandably different perspective: '*In Search of Excellence* was the first book written about things that work. It was purposeful. Hayes and Abernathy trashed American management and wrote it in the Harvard manual. Admittedly, the logic of the book was that American management was screwed up. It was a brutal, upfront attack on American management and McKinsey thinking. Okay it was 75 percent about islands of hope but that was what they were: exceptional. I consider *In Search of Excellence* a bad news book.'[1]

For such a trailblazing book, *In Search of Excellence* is, in retrospect at least, surprisingly uncontroversial. Peters and Waterman admit that what they have to say is not particularly original. But, they also have the insight to observe that the ideas they were espousing had been generally left behind, ignored or overlooked by management theorists.

The book emerged from research carried out by Peters and Waterman with the consulting firm, McKinsey, where both worked. The research identified excellent companies and then sought to distill lessons from their behavior and performance. Eventually, the sample was distilled down to 62 companies (with the rider that they were not intended to be perfectly representative).

The choices were largely uncontroversial and unsurprising – including the likes of IBM, Hewlett-Packard, Wal-Mart and General Electric. The emphasis was exclusively on big companies.

'*Search* was an out-and-out attack on the excesses of the "rational model" and the "business strategy paradigm" that had come to dominate Western management thinking. What it counseled instead was a return to first principles: attention to customers ('close to the customer'), an abiding concern for people ('productivity through people'), and the celebration of trial and error ('a bias for action'),' wrote Peters in his later book *Liberation Management*. 'But whether or not Bob Waterman and I were on management's case or on its side, there are more important fish to fry. To wit, an enormous error that resided between the lines: While *Search* condemned the excesses of dispassionate "modern management practice", it nonetheless celebrated big manufacturing businesses. With the exaltation of IBM and more than one nod to GM, we implicitly endorsed the humongous American technocratic enterprise in general – the institutions that economist John Kenneth Galbraith and business historian Alfred Chandler had not so long before declared almost perfect instruments for achieving America's economic manifest destiny. Make no mistake, Bob Waterman and I, who came of age in the '50s and '60s, were Galbraith's and Chandler's offspring!'

While the book celebrates the successful techniques employed by large companies many of the techniques are more easily and successfully employed by smaller companies. This also explains the book's perennial appeal.

During their research Peters and Waterman, aided by Harvard's Anthony Athos and Richard Pascale (authors of *The Art of Japanese Management*), developed a framework which was labeled the Seven Ss (or the 'mighty atom'). This proved highly influential (and is covered in detail in the section on *The Art of Japanese Management*).

Perhaps more usefully, the conclusions from Peters and

Waterman's work are distilled down into eight crucial characteristics. These have largely stood the test of time:

- **a bias for action** – 'Do it, fix it, try it, is our favorite axiom,' write Peters and Waterman.
- **close to the customer** – 'The excellent companies really are close to their customers. That's it. Other companies talk about it; the excellent companies do it,' they say. Later they add the 'smart-dumb rule' – 'Many of today's managers – MBA-trained and their like – may be a little bit too smart for their own good. The smart ones are the ones who shift direction all the time, based upon the latest output from the expected value equation. The ones who juggle hundred-variable models with facility; the ones who design complicate incentive systems; the ones who wire up matrix structures. The ones who have 200-page strategic plans and 500-page market requirement documents that are but one step in product development exercises. Our dumber friends are different. They just don't understand why every customer can't get personalized service, even in the potato chip business.'
- **autonomy and entrepreneurship** – the excellent companies encourage and nurture an entrepreneurial spirit among all employees.
- **productivity through people** – Peters and Waterman quote a GM worker laid off after 16 years making Pontiacs: 'I guess I was laid off because I make poor quality cars. But in 16 years, not once was I ever asked for a suggestion as to how to do my job better. Not once.'
- **hands-on values driven** – 'It appears that the real role of the chief executive is to manage the values of the organization,' conclude Peters and Waterman. Executives nurture and sustain corporate values. Rather than being distant figureheads, they are there making things

happen – 'The word manager in lip service institutions often has come to mean not someone who rolls up his or her sleeves to get the job done right alongside the worker, but someone who hires assistants to do it.'

- **stick to the knitting** – the excellent companies remained fixated on what they know they are good at and are not easily distracted.
- **simple form, lean staff** – 'One of the key attributes of the excellent companies is that they have realized the importance of keeping things simple despite over-whelming genuine pressures to complicate things,' write Peters and Waterman.
- **simultaneous loose-tight properties** – here, Peters and Waterman, are probably at their weakest and vaguest. The debate about how to become loose and tight (controlled and empowered; big yet small) has dominated much of the subsequent business writing. More recently it has tended to be explained as the essentially paradoxical nature of management. 'We need to consider adding terms to our management vocabulary: a few might be temporary structures, ad hoc groups, fluid organizations, small is beautiful, incrementalism, experimentation, action orientation, imitations, lots of tries, unjustified variations, internal competition, playfulness, the technology of foolishness, product champions, bootlegging, skunk works, cabals, and shadow organizations. Each of these turns the tables on conventional wisdom. Each implies both the absence of clear directions and the simultaneous need for action,' they write in *In Search of Excellence*.

The formulae behind *In Search of Excellence* is open to criticism. The criteria for selection was debatable, as all criteria are, and set Peters and Waterman up for criticism when their excellent companies fell from grace. This happened sooner than they could have anticipated and, in 1984, *Business Week*'s cover story (under the headline 'Oops!') gleefully revealed that some of the excellent companies had speedily declined into mediocrity and, in some cases, abject failure. The good news was the book's Achilles heel though Peters and Waterman do provide a warning – 'We are asked how we know that the companies we have defined as culturally innovative will stay that way. The answer is we don't.'

The worth, or otherwise, of *In Search of Excellence* is now impossible to gauge. Its fame and success have outstripped objective judgements of the book's merits. What can be said is that it created the impetus for the deluge of business books and, in the business world, established customer service as a key form of differentiation and advantage.

Notes

1   Interview with Stuart Crainer, 17 June, 1996.

36

TOM PETERS

Liberation Management

1992

Hamel on Peters

"Though one might accuse Tom Peters of being more journalist than management scholar, *Liberation Management* previewed many of the themes that would come to occupy management thinkers in the 1990s. One might wish, though, that the ratio of insight to data were a bit higher, and that there were a few less case studies and a bit more conceptual structure. Nevertheless, the book remains a good, though overlong, introduction to new age management philosophy."

L arge, rambling and gushingly anecdotal, *Liberation Management*, is a sprawling compendium of Tom Peters' thinking on management in the 'nanosecond nineties'.

The original manuscript was 1,900 pages long and was only reduced to a manageable size after a third of the material was cut. It is, observed Karl Weick, written in 'hyper-text'. The language is colorful – 'middle managers, as we have known them, are cooked geese'; 'the definition of every product and service is hanging. Going soft, softer, softest. Going fickle, ephemeral, fashion' – and, at times, impenetrable as Peters' passion overwhelms his prose. *Liberation Management* received the best and worst reviews of Peters' six books.

Liberation Management marks an important development in Peters' career. It emerged from an intensive period of reading Chandler and Hayek and is the first of his books since *In Search of Excellence* to feature in-depth examinations of individual companies.

Liberation Management's central message reflects a substantial change of emphasis from that of Peters' earlier works (*In Search of Excellence*, *A Passion for Excellence* and *Thriving on Chaos*). Ten years on from *In Search of Excellence*, Peters contends that his previous work was marred by paying too little attention to the perennially vexed question of organizational structure.

Peters does not mean structure in the traditional hierarchical and functional sense. Indeed, his exemplars of the new organizational structure are notable for their apparent lack of structure. And herein lies Peters' point. Companies such as CNN, ABB and Body Shop thrive through having highly flexible structures able to change to meet the business needs of the moment. Freeflowing, impossible to pin down, unchartable, simple yet complex, these are the paradoxical structures of the future. 'Tomorrow's effective "organization" will be conjured up anew each day,' says Peters.

Only with such vibrant structures will companies be able

to deliver the customer service championed by Peters in his previous books and, it is only through such dynamic organizational forms that companies will be able to survive. Not that Peters forgets customer service. 'How customers perceive their relationship with your company determines whether or not you'll have a customer for life. That's almost obvious, if almost always ignored.'

Key to the new corporate structures envisaged by Peters are networks with customers, with suppliers and, indeed, anyone else who can help the business deliver. 'Old ideas about size must be scuttled. "New big", which can be very big indeed, is "network big". That is, size measured by market power, say, is a function of the firm's extended family of fleeting and semi-permanent cohorts, not so much a matter of what it owns and directly controls,' he writes.

And, networks must move quickly. The book's central refrain is that of fashion – 'We're all in Milan's haute couture business and Hollywood's movie business,' writes Peters. 'This book is animated by a single word: fashion. Life cycles of computers and microprocessors have shrunk from years to months.' The new model organization moves fast and continually does so, seeking out new areas which make it unique in its markets.

Clearly, this requires quite different managerial skills than those traditionally needed by managers. Indeed, Peters says that the new organizational forms he depicts are 'troublesome to conceive – and a downright pain to manage'. The new skills are now familiar. Peters bids farewell to command and control, ushering in a new era characterized by 'curiosity, initiative, and the exercise of imagination'. It is, he argues, a step into the unknown for most organizations but also a return to first principles: 'For the last 100 years or so ... we've assumed that there is one place where expertise should reside: with "expert" staffs at division, group, sector, or corporate. And another, very different, place where the (mere) work gets done. The new organization regimen puts expertise back, close to the action – as it was in craft-oriented, pre-industrial revolution days ... We are not, then, ignoring "expertise" at all. We are simply shifting its locus, expanding its reach, giving it new respect – and acknowledging that everyone must be an expert in a fast-paced, fashionized world.'

In his two subsequent books – *The Tom Peters Seminar* and *The Pursuit of Wow!* – Peters has developed the ideas in *Liberation Management* still further, advocating complete commitment to vibrant, free-wheeling organizational structures. Peters identifies *Liberation Management* as the best of his books. Its merits – and drawbacks – lie in its relentless energy and endless examples. Interestingly, many of the companies featured by Peters have been used as examples in a wide variety of later books.

37

MICHAEL PORTER

Competitive Strategy: Techniques for Analyzing Industries and Competitors

1980

Hamel on Porter

"Strategy is, above all else, the search for above average returns. In *Competitive Strategy*, Michael Porter did a masterful job of synthesizing all that economists know about what determines industry and firm profitability. While *Competitive Strategy* isn't much help in discovering profitable strategies, it is an unfailing guide to whether some particular strategy, once articulated, can be counted on to produce worthwhile profits. What distinguishes *Competitive Strategy* from many other contemporary business books is its strong conceptual foundation. Every MBA graduate in the world can remember Porter's 'five forces'. How many can recall the eight rules of excellence?**"**

Michael Porter

Michael Porter took a doctorate in business economics and an MBA. Precociously talented, he also has a degree in aeronautical engineering from Princeton; joined the Harvard faculty at the age of 26; and could have been a professional golfer (he now settles for rounds with the President). Born in 1947, Michael Porter is now a professor at Harvard Business School and the world's leading authority on competitive strategy. He is the author of 12 books and many articles. His most influential books have been *Competitive Strategy: Techniques for Analyzing Industries and Competitors* (1980); *Competitive Advantage: Creating and Sustaining Superior Performance* (1985); *Competition in Global Industries* (1986) and *The Competitive Advantage of Nations* (1990). 'If anyone is capable of turning management theory into a respectable scholarly discipline, it is Michael Porter,' noted *The Economist*.[1]

Porter has served as a counselor on competitive strategy to many leading US and international companies and plays an active role in economic policy with the US Congress, business groups and as an adviser to foreign governments. He serves on the executive committee of the Council on Competitiveness, a private sector group of business, labor and academic leaders formed in 1986.

M ichael Porter's *Competitive Strategy: Techniques for Analyzing Industries and Competitors* is a rationalist's solution to a long-running strategic dilemma. As with many other managerial dilemmas, this involves the opposite ends of a spectrum. At one end are the pragmatists who contend that companies have to respond to their own specific situation. To them, competitive advantage emerges from immediate, fast thinking responsiveness. As every situation is unique there is no pat formula by which sustainable competitive advantage can be achieved. At the other end of the spectrum is the line taken by, among others, the Boston Consulting Group. They suggest that market knowledge is all-important. Any company which masters the intricacies of a particular market will be well placed to reduce prices and increase market share.

Porter proposes a logical compromise, arguing that there are three 'generic strategies', 'viable approaches to dealing with ... competitive forces'. Strategy, in Porter's eyes, is distilled down to a choice on *how* to compete. (Interestingly, Porter has said that the idea of generic strategies was a late addition to the book.)

The first generic strategy is differentiation, competing on the basis of value added to customers (quality, service, differentiation) so that customers will pay a premium to cover higher costs. The second is cost-based leadership, offering products or services at the lowest cost. Quality and service are not unimportant, but cost reduction provides focus to the organization. Focus is the third generic strategy identified by Porter. Companies with a clear strategy outperform those whose strategy is unclear or those which attempt to achieve both differentiation and cost leadership. 'Sometimes the firm can successfully pursue more than one approach as its primary target, though this is rarely possible,' says Porter. 'Effectively implementing any of these generic strategies usually requires total commitment, and organizational arrangements are diluted if there's more than one primary target.'

If a company fails to focus on any of the three generic strategies it is liable to encounter problems. 'The firm failing to develop its strategy in at least one of the three directions – a firm that is "stuck in the middle" – is in an extremely poor strategic situation,' Porter writes. 'The firm lacks the market share, capital investment, and resolve to play the low-cost game, the industry-wide differentiation necessary to obviate the need for a low-cost position, or the focus to create differentiation or low cost in a more limited sphere. The firm stuck in the middle is almost guaranteed low profitability. It either loses the high-volume customers who demand low prices or must bid away its profits to get this business away from low-cost firms. Yet it also loses high-margin businesses – the cream – to the firms who are focused on high-margin targets or have achieved differentiation overall. The firm stuck in the middle also probably suffers from a blurred corporate culture and a conflicting set of organizational arrangements and motivation system.'

When *Competitive Strategy* was published, in 1980, Porter's generic strategies offered a rational and straightforward method of companies extricating themselves from strategic confusion. The reassurance proved short-lived. Less than a decade later, companies were having to compete on all fronts. They had to be differentiated, through improved service or speedier development, and be cost leaders, cheaper than their competitors.

Porter's other contribution in *Competitive Strategy* has proved more robust. 'In any industry, whether it is domestic or international or produces a product or a service, the rules of competition are embodied in five competitive forces,' he writes.

1 **The entry of new competitors**
   New competitors necessitate some competitive response which will inevitably use some of your resources, thus reducing profits.

2 **The threat of substitutes**
   If there are viable alternatives to your product or service in the marketplace, the prices you can charge will be limited.

3 **The bargaining power of buyers**
   If customers have bargaining power they will use it. This will reduce profit margins and, as a result, affect profitability.

4 **The bargaining power of suppliers**
   Given power over you, suppliers will increase their prices and adversely affect your profitability.

5 **The rivalry among the existing competitors**
   Competition leads to the need to invest in marketing, R&D or price reductions, which will reduce your profits.

'The collective strength of these five competitive forces determines the ability of firms in an industry to earn, on average, rates of return on investment in excess of the cost of capital. The strength of the five forces varies from industry to industry, and can change as an industry evolves,' Porter observes.

The five forces outlined in *Competitive Strategy* are a means by which a company can begin to understand its particular industry. Initially, they were passively interpreted as valid statements of the facts of competitive life. Now, however, they are more regularly interpreted as the rules of the game which have to be changed and challenged if an organization is to achieve any impact in a particular market.

Notes
1   'Professor Porter PhD', *The Economist*, 8 October, 1994.

38

MICHAEL PORTER

The Competitive Advantage of Nations

1990

Hamel on Porter

"While *The Competitive Advantage of Nations* provides a good account of why particular industry 'clusters' emerged in some countries and not others, it is essentially backward looking. In a world of open markets, and mobile capital, technology and knowledge, no firm need be the product of its geography. That a German company, SAP, can succeed in the software industry; that a Japanese company, Yamaha, can lead the world in making grand pianos, and a Korean company, Samsung, can become number one in the world in memory semiconductors suggests that geography is having less and less to do with firm competitiveness. *The Competitive Advantage of Nations* was a wonderful historical study and was certainly useful to governments to construct policy that promoted the competitiveness of indigenous firms, but it told us almost nothing about the future of competitiveness – a future in which companies from one part of the world can access and internalize the competitive advantage of far distant geographies.**"**

ichael Porter's *The Competitive Advantage of Nations* is one of the most ambitious books of our times. Tom Peters, an unlikely bedfellow for the ultrarational Porter, called it 'magisterial'. At its heart is a radical new perspective of the role and *raison d'être* of nations. From being military powerhouses they are now economic units whose competitiveness is the key to power.

The book emerged from Porter's work on Ronald Reagan's Commission on Industrial Competitiveness. 'The book that projected Mr. Porter into the stratosphere, read by aspiring intellectuals and despairing politicians everywhere, was *The Competitive Advantage of Nations*,' said *The Economist*. 'This work can be read on three levels: as a general inquiry into what makes national economies successful, as a detailed study of eight of the world's main modern economies, and as a series of prescriptions about what governments should do to improve their country's competitiveness.'[1]

Porter's research, in fact, encompasses ten countries: the UK, Denmark, Italy, Japan, Korea, Singapore, Sweden, Switzerland, the US and Germany (then West Germany). Porter seeks to build on the ideas of his previous books to examine what makes a nation's firms and industries competitive in global markets and what propels a whole nation's economy to advance. 'Why are firms based in a particular nation able to create and sustain competitive advantage against the world's best competitors in a particular field? And why is one nation often the home for so many of an industry's world leaders?' asks Porter. 'Why is tiny Switzerland the home base for international leaders in pharmaceuticals, chocolate and trading? Why are leaders in heavy trucks and mining equipment based in Sweden?'

Porter returns to first principles, an ambitious move in itself given the nature of the nationalistic minefield he ventures in to. 'The principal economic goal of a nation is to produce a high and rising standard of living for its citizens. The ability to do so depends not on the amorphous notion of "competitiveness" but on the productivity with which a nation's resources (labor and capital) are employed,' he writes. 'Productivity is the prime determinant in the long run of a nation's standard of living.'

Unlike Kenichi Ohmae who champions the 'end of the nation state', Porter's research leads to different conclusions. He identifies a central paradox. Companies and industries have become globalized and more international in their scope and aspirations than ever before. This, on the surface at least, would appear to suggest that the nation has lost its role in the international success of its firms. 'Companies, at first glance, seem to have transcended countries. Yet what I have learned in this study contradicts this conclusion,' says Porter. 'While globalization of competition might appear to make the nation less important, instead it seems to make it more so. With fewer impediments to trade to shelter uncompetitive domestic firms and industries, the home nation takes on growing significance because it is the source of the skills and technology that underpin competitive advantage.'

Porter also lays down a challenge, perhaps to himself, to solve another perennial mystery: 'Much is known about what competitive advantage is and how particular actions create or destroy it. Much else is known about why a company makes good choices instead of bad choices in seeking bases for competitive advantage, and why some firms are more aggressive in pursuing them.'

Porter's conclusion is that it is the intensity of domestic competition which often fuels success on a global stage.

To make sense of the dynamics behind national or regional strength in a particular industry, Porter develops the national 'diamond'. This is made up of four forces:

1 **Factor conditions**
   These once would have include natural resources and plentiful supplies of labor; now they embrace data communications, university research and the avail-

ability of scientists, engineers or experts in a particular field.

2 **Demand conditions**

If there is strong national demand for a product or service this can give the industry a headstart in global competition. The US, for example, is ahead in health services due to heavy national demand.

3 **Related and supporting industries**

These are industries which are strong in particular countries are often surrounded by successful related industries.

4 **Firm strategy, structure and rivalry**

Domestic competition fuels growth and competitive strength.

Notes

1   'Professor Porter PhD', *The Economist*, 8 October 1994.

39

EDGAR H. SCHEIN

Organizational Culture and Leadership

1985

Hamel on Schein

"It is impossible to change a large organization without first understanding that organization's culture. Ed Schein gave us an ability to look deeply into what makes an organization what it is, thus providing the foundation of any successful effort at 'transformation' or 'change'. *Organizational Culture and Leadership* remains essential reading for all aspiring 'change agents'."

Edgar H. Schein

Edgar H. Schein studied social psychology at Stanford and then at Harvard. He is now professor of management at Massachusetts Institute of Technology. The roots of his thinking can be traced back to early influences on his career including Douglas McGregor, Warren Bennis and Chris Argyris. Schein taught and profoundly influenced, among others, Charles Handy.

More recently, his work on the 'psychological contract' and his concept of 'career anchors' has attracted attention. Schein believes we have a single 'career anchor', the underlying career value which we are unwilling to surrender.

E dgar Schein's 1985 book *Organizational Culture and Leadership* paved the way for a plethora of studies of corporate culture. Indeed, Schein is sometimes seen as the inventor of the term 'corporate culture'- and, at the very least, one of its originators.

Schein describes culture as 'a pattern of basic assumptions – invented, discovered, or developed by a given group as it learns to cope with its problems of external adaptation and internal integration – that has worked well enough to be considered valid and, therefore, to be taught to new members as the correct way to perceive, think, and feel in relation to those problems'. Instead of regarding everything an organization does as part of its culture, Schein takes a more psychological view. Schein's 'basic assumptions' are re-phrased and reinterpreted elsewhere in a variety of ways – perhaps the nearest is Chris Argyris' term 'theories-in-use'.

These basic assumptions, says Schein, can be categorized into five dimensions:

1 **Humanity's relationship to nature** While some companies regard themselves as masters of their own destiny, others are submissive, willing to accept the domination of their external environment.

2 **The nature of reality and truth** Organizations and managers adopt a wide variety of methods to reach what becomes accepted as the organizational 'truth' – through debate, dictatorship, or through simple acceptance that if something achieves the objective it is right.

3 **The nature of human nature** Organizations differ in their views of human nature. Some follow McGregor's Theory X and work on the principle that people will not do the job if they can avoid it. Others regard people in more positive light and attempt to enable them to fulfill their potential for the benefit of both sides.

4 **The nature of human activity** The West has traditionally emphasized tasks and their completion rather than the more philosophical side of work. Achievement is all. Schein suggests an alternative approach – 'being-in-becoming' – emphasizing self-fulfillment and development.

5 **The nature of human relationships** Organizations make a variety of assumptions about how people interact with each other. Some facilitate social interaction, while others regard it as an unnecessary distraction.

These five categories are not mutually exclusive, but are in a constant state of development and flux. Culture does not stand still.

Key to the creation and development of corporate culture are the values embraced by the organization. Schein acknowledges that a single person can shape these values and, as a result, an entire corporate culture. (This spawned a wave of interest in the heroic creators of corporate cultures from Henry Ford to IBM's Thomas Watson.) Schein identifies three stages in the development of a corporate culture.

In the first, 'birth and early growth' the culture may be dominated by the business founder. The culture is regarded as a source of the company's identity, a bonding agent protecting it against outside forces.

In the next stage, 'organizational mid-life', the original culture is likely to be diluted and undermined as new cultures emerge and there is a loss of the original sense of identity. At this stage, there is an opportunity for the fundamental culture to be realigned and changed.

If this fails to happen the culture moves to the final stage, 'organizational maturity', where it is a burden. Culture, at this stage, is regarded sentimentally. People are hopelessly addicted to how things used to be done and unwilling to contemplate change. Here the organization is at its weakest, as the culture has been transformed from a source of competitive advantage and distinctiveness to a hindrance in the marketplace. Only through aggressive measures will it survive.

Importantly each stage of the culture's growth requires a different method of change. If culture is to work in support of a company's strategy, Schein believes there has to be a level of consensus covering five areas:

- the core mission or primary task
- goals
- the means to accomplish the goals
- how to measure progress
- remedial or repair strategies.

Schein regards achieving cultural change as a formidable challenge, one that well-established executives in strong cultures often find beyond them. The exceptional executives who achieve cultural change from within a culture they are closely identified with (such as GE's Jack Welch) are rarities, and are labeled by Schein as cultural 'hybrids'.

Organizational Culture and Leadership clarified the entire area of corporate culture in a way no-one previously had achieved. Its perspectives on culture as a constantly changing force in corporate life remain valuable though disconcerting – it begins to feel as if culture has a life of its own and only exceptional people or extraordinary actions can disturb its momentum.

40

RICARDO SEMLER

Maverick!

1993

Hamel on Semler

"Almost none of the great management books that populate this volume were written by practicing managers. Why is this? Perhaps it is because managers seldom have the time, or the perspective, to generalize from their own experiences. Books by Lee Iacocca, Harold Geneen, and other management icons are typically as idiosyncratic as they are entertaining. While the managerial 'solutions' espoused by Ricardo Semler may not be universally applicable, the set of beliefs that animate his particular approach are clearly laid out and can be debated on their own merits. Semler's book rises above the genre because it is more than a catalog of self-congratulatory anecdotes; it deals, in a very novel way, with deep questions of management."

Ricardo Semler

In 1990 and again in 1992, **Ricardo Semler** – majority owner of a Sao Paulo manufacturing company, Semco S/A, which specializes in marine and food-service equipment – was elected business leader of the year by a poll of 52,000 Brazilian executives. His book *Maverick!* is an international bestseller. In Brazil it was on the bestseller list for 200 weeks.

Semler has studied at Harvard Business School and has written articles for the *Harvard Business Review*. He was Vice-President of the Federation of Industries of Brazil and is a member of the board of SOS Atlantic Forest, Brazil's foremost environmental organization.

R icardo Semler's *Maverick!* is one of the most surprising business bestsellers of recent times. Prior to its publication the thought of learning managerial lessons from a Brazilian corporation was risible. Today, with *Maverick!* having sold one million copies, Semler's unique managerial style has been consumed by managers throughout the world.

In 1980 Semler took over his family's company, Semco, from his father. The company was unexceptional in performance and management. Given two to three weeks to change things, Semler set about restructuring it in a dramatic and revolutionary fashion. In a single day he fired 60 percent of the company's top management. He based his revolution on three values: employee participation, profit sharing and open information systems. 'In these days of the new world order, almost everyone believes people have a right to vote for those who lead them, at least in the public sector,' writes Semler. 'But democracy has yet to penetrate the work place. Dictators and despots are alive and well in offices and factories all over the world.'

Take Semco's reaction to a dramatic situation. In 1990 the Brazilian minister of finance effectively seized 80 percent of the nation's cash. The economy entered a state of chaotic paralysis. At Semco, sales were reduced to zero. The company had $4 million of products which its customers simply could not pay for. Costs were slashed in an attempt to stay afloat. Then, gathering the company's employees together, possible solutions were discussed. The employees agreed to a 30 percent wage cut so long as their profit sharing was increased from 24 percent to 39 percent and providing managers took a 40 percent pay cut. The final element of the agreement was that a member of the union committee signed every check issued by the company.

It is difficult to imagine such an agreement being considered in any other organization, let alone accepted. Semler used it as a means of accelerating the pace of change – if

Semco's 850 employees were so committed and so willing to seek out imaginative solutions to the company's problems in a crisis, why couldn't their ingenuity be harnessed all the time?

Semco now has just four grades of staff. The job of chief executive is handled by six senior managers for six months at a time (Semler is one of them). Managers set their own salaries and bonuses and are evaluated by those who work for them. Employees decide their own working hours, set quotas and improve products and processes. 'The company is organized – well, maybe that's not quite the right word for us – not to depend too much on any individual, especially me,' writes Semler. 'I take it as a point of pride that twice on my return from long trips my office had been moved – and each time it got smaller. My role is that of a catalyst. I try to create an environment in which others make decisions. Success means not making them myself.'

Though Semler's message has been granted massive media attention, few have been brave enough to follow Semco's lead. Former BTR chief, Sir Owen Green, is typical of the dismissive reaction from mainstream business leaders claiming that Semler's 'not maverick; he is an eccentric'. Charles Handy is more positive: 'The way that Ricardo Semler runs his company is impossible; except that it works, and works splendidly for everyone.'

Maverick! is an exception to the general run of books by successful executives. There is none of the usual corporate heroism but, instead, an acceptance that management is concerned with enabling others rather than controlling them.

41

PETER SENGE

The Fifth Discipline: The Art and Practice of the Learning Organization

1990

Hamel on Senge

"Like Michael Porter, Peter Senge is a master of synthesis. Like Chris Argyris and Ed Schein, he tackles the deep structure of problems, not their superficial manifestations. While Professor Argyris put organizational learning on the management agenda, Peter Senge married it with system thinking and created a language and approach that makes the whole set of ideas accessible to managers. Peter is no mere theorist, his Organizational Learning Center at MIT has helped launch thousands of in-company learning experiments. *The Fifth Discipline* would certainly be on my shortlist of the half dozen best business books of the last 25 years."

Peter Senge

Peter Senge (born 1947) is director of the Center for Organizational Learning at the Massachusetts institute of Technology. He graduated in engineering from Stanford before doing a Ph.D. on social systems modeling at MIT.

Senge studies how firms and other organizations can develop adaptive capabilities in a world of increasing complexity and rapid change. In his book *The Fifth Discipline: The Art and Practice of the Learning Organization* he gives managers tools and conceptual archetypes to help them understand the structures and dynamics underlying their organizations' problems.

eter Senge's *The Fifth Discipline: The Art and Practice of the Learning Organization* popularized the concept of the learning organization.

'As the world becomes more interconnected and business becomes more complex and dynamic, work must become more *learningful*,' writes Senge. 'It is no longer sufficient to have one person learning for the organization, a Ford or a Sloan or a Watson. It's just not possible any longer to "figure it out" from the top, and have everybody else following the orders of the "grand strategist". The organizations that will truly excel in the future will be the organizations that discover how to tap people's commitment and capacity to learn at all levels in an organization.'

Senge argues that managers should encourage employees to be open to new ideas, communicate frankly with each other, understand thoroughly how their companies operate, form a collective vision and work together to achieve their goal. In the learning organization managers will become researchers and designers rather than controllers and overseers.

Though Senge's book was a bestseller and the idea of the learning organization became fashionable, *The Fifth Discipline* emerged from extensive research. Senge and his team at the Center for Organizational Learning at MIT's Sloan School of Management have been working on the theme for some time. 'For the past 15 years or longer, many of us have been struggling to understand what "learning organizations" are all about, and how to make progress in moving organizations along this path. Out of these efforts, I believe some insights are emerging,' says Senge in the multi-authored sequel, *The Fifth Discipline Fieldbook: Strategies and Tools for Building a Learning Organization*.

In *The Fifth Discipline*, Senge suggests that there are five components to a learning organization:

1 **Systems thinking** Senge introduces the idea of systems archetypes, in practical terms this can help man-

agers spot repetitive patterns, such as the way certain kinds of problems persist, or the way systems have their own in-built limits to growth. Senge champions systems thinking, recognizing that things are interconnected. He regards corporations as complex systems. This has pushed managerial thinking towards contemplating complexity theory which has spawned numerous books though few go beyond the basic metaphor. (Ralph Stacey's *Complexity and Creativity in Organizations* is one of the few to develop from Senge's ideas. Stacey argues that creativity 'is inevitably messy' and 'to remove that mess by inspiring us to follow some common vision, share the same culture and pull together, is to remove ... the raw material of creative activity'.)

2 **Personal mastery** Senge grounds this idea in the familiar competencies and skills associated with management, but also includes spiritual growth – opening oneself up to a progressively deeper reality – and living life from a creative rather than a reactive viewpoint. This discipline involves two underlying movements – continually learning how to see current reality more clearly – and the ensuing gap between vision and reality produces the creative tension from which learning arises. 'In the simplest sense, a learning organization is a group of people who are continually enhancing their capability to create their future,' says Senge. 'The traditional meaning of the word *learning* is much deeper than just *taking information in*. It is about changing individuals so that they produce results they care about, accomplish things that are important to them.'[1]

3 **Mental models** This essentially deals with the organization's driving and fundamental values and principles. Senge alerts managers to the power of patterns of thinking at the organizational level and the importance of non-defensive inquiry into the nature of these patterns.

4 **Shared vision** Here Senge stresses the importance of co-creation and argues that shared vision can only be built on personal vision. He claims that shared vision is present when the task that follows from the vision is no longer seen by the team members as separate from the self.

5 **Team learning** The discipline of team learning involves two practices: dialogue and discussion. The former is characterized by its exploratory nature, the latter by the opposite process of narrowing down the field to the best alternative for the decisions that need to be made. The two are mutually complimentary, but the benefits of combining them only come from having previously separated them. Most teams lack the ability to distinguish between the two and to move consciously between them.

In practice corporate habits are hard to break. 'I know people who've lost their jobs supporting these theories,' Senge later admitted. 'Yet they go on. One man told me that by adopting the learning organization model, he'd made what he called "job limiting choices". What he meant was that he could have climbed the corporate ladder faster by rejecting my theories and toeing the company line. But what would that have brought him? A higher pension fund and more stock, maybe. That's not what matters.'[2]

Transforming companies into learning organizations has proved highly problematical. The principle reason for this is that it involves managers surrendering their traditional spheres of power and control. They have to hand over power to the people who are learning and, if people are to learn, they must be allowed to experiment and fail. In a blame-oriented culture, this requires a major change in attitude.

Senge's concept of the learning organization demands trust and involvement. Again, this is usually notable by its absence. 'Real commitment is rare in today's organizations. It is our experience that 90 percent of the time what passes for commitment is compliance,' writes Senge.

'Perhaps the problem is that although the learning organization sounds as if it is a product, it is actually a process. Processes are not suddenly unveiled for all to see,' says Phil Hodgson of the UK's Ashridge Management College. 'Academic definitions, no matter how precise, cannot be instantly applied in the real world. Managers need to promote learning so that it gradually emerges as a key part of an organization's culture. Being convinced of the merits of the learning organization is not usually a matter of dramatic conversion.'

Even so, *The Fifth Discipline* has proved highly influential. Though the learning organization has rarely been converted into reality, the idea has fueled the debate on self-managed development, employability and has affected the rewards and remuneration strategies of many organizations.

Notes

1 Quoted in Napuk, K, 'Live and learn', *Scottish Business Insider*, January 1994.
2 Quoted in Griffith, V, 'Corporate fashion victim', *Financial Times*, 12 April, 1995.

42

ALFRED P. SLOAN

My Years with General Motors

1963

Hamel on Sloan

"Can you be big and nimble? The question is as timely today as it was when Sloan took over General Motors. Despite divisionalization and decentralization, Sloan's organizational inventions, GM still fell victim to its size. Though, perhaps, size was simply a metaphor for success. Was it bigness that made GM vulnerable, or the arrogance and sense of invincibility that came with years of success? One thing is certain, the corporate superstructure that emerged to manage GM's independent divisions was more successful in creating bureaucracy than in exploiting cross-divisional synergies. The challenge of achieving divisional autonomy and flexibility on one hand, while reaping the benefits of scale and coordination on the other, is one that has eluded not only GM, but many other large companies as well.**"**

Alfred P. Sloan (1875-1966)

Alfred P. Sloan, the legendary chief of General Motors, was one of the first managers to write an important theoretical book.

Sloan was General Manager of the Hyatt Roller Bearing Company at the age of 24 and became President when it merged with United Motors which, in turn, became part of General Motors in 1917. Initially a director and Vice-President, Sloan became GM's Chief Executive in 1946 and honorary Chairman from 1956 until his death.

M *y Years With General Motors* is Alfred P. Sloan's account of his remarkable career. It is, however, an often turgid testimony to Sloan's achievements. 'His book is one thing, what he did at GM is quite another,' says London Business School's Sumantra Ghoshal. 'Sloan created a new organizational form – the multi-divisional form – which became a doctrine of management. Today, it is not ascribed to him, but Sloan was its instigator.'

When Alfred P. Sloan took over General Motors the fledgling automobile market was dominated by Ford. Under Henry Ford the company had become a pioneer of mass production techniques. In 1920 Ford was making a car a minute and the famous black Model T accounted for 60 percent of the market. General Motors managed to scrimp and scrap its way to around 12 percent.

With Ford cornering the mass market, the accepted wisdom was that the only alternative for competitors lay in the negligibly-sized luxury market. Sloan thought otherwise and concentrated GM's attentions on the, as yet non-existent, middle market. His aim was a car for 'every purse and every purpose'.

At the time, GM was an unwieldy combination of companies with eight models which basically competed against each other as well as against Ford. Sloan cut the eight models down to five and decided that rather than competing with each other, each model would be targeted at a particular segment of the market. The five GM ranges – the Chevrolet, Oldsmobile, Pontiac, Buick and Cadillac – were to be updated and changed regularly and came in more than one color. Ford continued to offer functional, reliable cars; GM offered choice.

While all this made commercial sense, Sloan inherited an organization which was ill-suited to deliver his aspirations. GM had been built up through the regular and apparently random acquisition of small companies. Any thought of providing some sort of overall corporate culture, structure or direction had apparently been overlooked – though this was principally because it had never been done before.

Sloan set about creating a coherent organization from his motley collection. Central to this was his 'organization study' which, said one observer, appeared to 'have sprung entirely from his own head in 1919 and 1920'. In the early 1920s Sloan organized the company into eight divisions – five car divisions and three component divisions. In the jargon (invented 50 years later) they were strategic business units.

Each was made responsible for all their commercial operations with their own engineering, production and sales departments, but was supervised by a central staff responsible for overall policy and finance. The operating units were semi-autonomous, charged with maintaining market share and sustaining profitability in their particular area. Alfred Chandler describes the system in *Strategy and Structure*: 'The responsibility attached to the chief executive of each operation shall in no way be limited. Each such organization headed by its chief executive shall be complete in every necessary function and enable to exercise its full initiative and logical development'. In a particularly innovative move, the components divisions not only sold products to other GM companies, but also to external companies.

This policy of, what Sloan labeled, 'federal decentralization' marked the invention of the decentralized, divisionalized organization. (While this was its first sustained practical usage, Sloan's ideas can be traced back to Henri Fayol's functional approach.) 'Alfred Sloan did for the upper layers of management what Henry Ford did for the shopfloor: he turned it into a reliable, efficient, machine-like process,' recently observed *The Economist*.[1]

The multi-divisional form enabled Sloan to utilize the company's size without making it cumbersome. Executives had more time to concentrate on strategic issues and operational decisions were made by people in the front line rather than at a distant headquarters. It required a continuous balancing act. 'In practically all our activities we seem to suffer from the inertia resulting from our great size,' commented Sloan in the 1930s. 'There are so many people involved and it requires such a tremendous effort to put something new into effect that a new idea is likely to be considered insignificant in comparison with the effort that it take to put it across... Sometimes I am almost forced to the conclusion that General Motors is so large and its inertia so great that it is impossible for us to be leaders.'

By 1925, with its new organization and commitment to annual changes in its models, GM had overtaken Ford which continued to persist with its faithful old Model T. Sloan's segmentation of the market changed the structure of the car industry – and provided a model for how firms could do the same in other industries.

Human interest in *My Years with General Motors* is limited. The then powerful unions are ignored. So, too, are key figures such as Charles Kettering (who invented the self-starter) and William Olds (of Oldsmobile). At first glance such omissions are not altogether surprising. Sloan's system, aimed to eliminate, as far as was possible, the deficiencies and eccentricities of managerial behavior. 'It is perhaps the most impersonal book of memoirs ever written,' observed Peter Drucker in his *Concept of the Corporation*. 'And this was clearly intentional. Sloan's book ... knows only one dimension: that of managing a business so that it can produce effectively, provide jobs, create markets and sales, and generate profits.'

And yet, Sloan was committed to what at the time would have been regarded as progressive human resource management. In 1947 Sloan established GM's employee-research section to look at employee attitudes and he invested a large amount of his own time in selecting the right people for the job – Sloan personally selected every GM executive from managers to master mechanics and, though he was prepared to miss policy meetings, he always attended personnel meetings.

Sloan established GM as a benchmark of corporate might, a symbol of American strength and success – 'What's good for GM is good for America,' ran the popular mythology. Peter Drucker and Alfred Chandler celebrated Sloan's approach. His legacy was unquestionably long-lasting – within GM at least. Researching her case study of GM for *The Change Masters*, Rosabeth Moss Kanter was told by then GM chairman Roger Smith that his aim was to 'return this company to the way Sloan intended it to be managed'.

Such nostalgia was self-defeating. The deficiencies of Sloan's model have gradually become apparent since the publication of his book. This was most obviously manifested in the decline of GM. The decentralized structure built up by Sloan revolved around a reporting and committee infrastructure which eventually became unwieldy. As time went by, more and more committees were set up. Stringent targets and narrow measures of success stultified initiative.

Sumantra Ghoshal and Christopher Bartlett have pointed to the inward-looking nature of Sloan's approach as one of its major drawbacks. 'Sloan's organization was designed to overcome the limitations of the functional structure in managing large, established businesses. While it did this quite well, at least for a while, it proved incapable of creating and developing new businesses internally. This inability to manage organic expansion into new areas was caused by many factors. With primarily operating responsibilities and guided by a measurement system that focused on profit and market share performance in served markets, the front-line business unit managers in the divisionalized corporation were neither expected to nor could scout for new opportunities breaking around the boxes in the organization chart that defined their product or geographic scope. Besides, small new ventures, as organic developments tended to be at the start of their lives, could not absorb the large central overheads and yet return the profits needed to justify the financial and human investments.'

By the end of the 1960s the delicate balance, which Sloan had brilliantly maintained between centralization and decentralization, was lost – finance emerged as the dominant function – and GM became paralyzed by what had once made it great.

Alfred P. Sloan is one of the very few figures who undoubtedly changed the world of management. Henry Ford regarded managers as mere supervisors. In contrast, at decentralized GM, senior executives were charged with three key roles. They had responsibility for the company's strategy; they designed its structure and selected its control systems. This relied on a steady, evenly paced supply of information from below. It is a model which has spawned a host of imitators.

Notes

1 'The changing nature of leadership', *The Economist*, 10 June, 1995.

43

ADAM SMITH

The Wealth of Nations

1776

Hamel on Smith

"Revisionists be damned. Citizens from Prague to Santiago to Guangzhou to Jakarta owe much of their new found prosperity to the triumph of Adam Smith's economic ideals. Adam Smith laid the philosophical foundations for the modern industrial economy. Enough said."

Adam Smith (1723–1790)

Born in Kirkcaldy, Scotland, **Adam Smith** entered the University of Glasgow at the age of 14. Strongly influenced by the university's professor of moral philosophy, Smith went to Balliol College, Oxford in 1740 and began to concentrate on moral philosophy. He returned to Scotland in 1746 and later joined Glasgow University as a Professor of Logic and then of moral philosophy.

Smith's writing career began in the 1750s and in 1759 he published his *Theory of Moral Sentiments*. After leaving the university in 1763, Smith spent time in France where he met leading thinkers including Voltaire. There is some evidence to suggest that Smith's *Inquiry into the Nature and Causes of the Wealth of Nations* was begun in Toulouse. The bulk, however, was written on Smith's return to Scotland. In 1773 he took his manuscript to London where he began to live. When it was published in 1776, *The Wealth of Nations* was instantly successful and influential. Lord North's budget in 1777 and 1778 was influenced by Smith.

Smith returned to Scotland where he worked as a tax collector and oversaw the destruction of most of his papers before his death in 1790 after a long illness.

dam Smith occupies a unique place in business and economic history. He is proclaimed as the champion of market forces, the patron saint of free enterprise. His reputation has been hijacked by politicians.

Academics and economists are increasingly skeptical about Smith's legacy. In his two volume history of economic thinking *Economic Thought before Adam Smith and Classical Economics*, Murray Rothbard debunks much of the Smith mythology. Rothbard labels Smith's theory of economic value an 'unmitigated disaster' and his 'labor theory of value' as a 'colossal blunder'.

In *The Wealth of Nations*, Smith contends that the value of a particular good or service is determined by the costs of production. If something is expensive to produce, then its value is similarly high. 'What is bought with money or with goods is purchased by labor, as much as what we acquire by the toil of our own body . . . They contain the value of a certain quantity of labor which we exchange for what is supposed at the time to contain the value of an equal quantity,' writes Smith.

This notion of what constitutes economic value is now a relic of a bygone age. In the age of the knowledge worker, labor is a misleading and elusive term. In modern manufacturing companies labor typically amounts to around 10 to 12 percent of total costs with 50 percent being spent on materials. And, Smith ignores the less quantifiable and mysterious valuations placed on goods and services by consumers. (Smith does not totally overlook the role of consumers and, in one contemporary-sounding paragraph observes: 'The pretense that corporations are necessary for the better government of the trade is without any foundation. The real and effectual discipline which is exercised over a workman is not that of his corporation, but that of his customers.')

Interestingly, Smith's theory can be seen as a stepping

stone towards Marxism. Marx observed that the industrial system 'converts the laborer into a crippled monstrosity, by forcing his detailed dexterity at the expense of a world of productive capabilities and instincts'. If the value generated by a product or service is directly related to the labor which goes into its creation, labor becomes the critical force in economics and should be nurtured rather than exploited. This is something which Smith acknowledges (though not necessarily his modern adherents) – 'The liberal reward of labor, therefore, as it is the necessary effect, so it is the natural symptom of increasing national wealth. The scanty maintenance of the laboring poor, on the other hand, is the natural symptom that things are at a standstill, and their starving condition that they are going fast backwards.'

In managerial terms, *The Wealth of Nations* laid the theoretical groundwork for the work of Frederick Taylor a century later. If labor denotes ultimate value, control and measurement of labor is vital, the principal route to increasing profitability. Smith writes: 'The division of labor ... occasions in every art, a proportionable increase of the productive powers of labor. The separation of different trades and employments from one another seems to have taken place in consequence of this advantage.'

Smith's message is that if you can cajole people to narrow their perspectives to the task in hand they are likely to become more productive. 'Men are much more likely to discover easier and readier methods of attaining any object when the whole attention of their minds is directed towards that single object than when it is dissipated among a great variety of things.'

Smith's legacy is still being debated and deconstructed. In *Reengineering the Corporation*, James Champy and Michael Hammer write: 'For two hundred years people have founded and built companies around Adam Smith's brilliant discovery that individual work should be broken down into its simplest and most basic tasks. In the post-industrial age we are now entering, corporations will be founded and built around the idea of reunifying those tasks into coherent business processes.'

In *The Wealth of Nations*, Smith has little time for managers and works on the principle that their motivation is purely selfish. Paradoxically, while managers and companies pursued a self-interested agenda, the good and betterment of society as a whole is maintained by the 'invisible hand' of the economy.

Maybe the most reasoned endorsement of Smith's work came from his fellow Scot, John Stuart Mill, who wrote in his preface to *Principles* (1865): 'Except on matters of detail there are perhaps no practical questions, even among those which approach nearest to the character of purely economic questions, which admit to being decided on economic premises alone. And it is because Adam Smith never loses sight of this truth, because in his applications of political economy he perpetually appeals to other and often far larger considerations than pure political economy affords, he gives that well-grounded feeling of command over the principles of the subject for purposes of practice, owing to which *The Wealth of Nations*, alone among treatises of political economy, has not only been popular with general readers, but has impressed itself strongly on the minds of men of the world and of legislators.' For all the talk of corporate and managerial revolution, it would be true to say that *The Wealth of Nations* continues to impress itself on the minds of many.

FREDERICK W. TAYLOR

The Principles of Scientific Management

1911

Hamel on Taylor

"The development of modern management theory is the story of two quests: to make management more scientific, and to make it more humane. It is wrong to look at the latter quest as somehow much more enlightened than the former. Indeed, they are the yin and yang of business. The unprecedented capacity of twentieth century industry to create wealth rests squarely on the work of Frederick Winslow Taylor. While some may disavow Taylor, his rational, deterministic impulses live on. Indeed, 1990s reengineering is simply late twentieth century Taylorism. Though the focus of reengineering is on the process, rather than the individual task, the motivation is the same: to simplify, to remove unnecessary effort, and to do more with less.**"**

Frederick W. Taylor (1856–1917)

A Philadelphia Quaker, **Frederick W. Taylor** was the quintessential brilliant Victorian. His interests were wide ranging and in virtually all he was highly successful. He was a tennis champion, changed the rules of baseball so that pitchers threw overarm rather than underarm and took out over 100 patents for his many and varied ideas. His inventiveness and his life's work were driven by a fundamental, sometimes blinding, belief in efficiency and measurement.

Taylor came from an affluent family and was educated in France and Germany. He worked as an apprentice at the Enterprise Hydraulic Works in Philadelphia in the 1870s and then at the Midvale Steel Company. At Midvale he became chief engineer and later general manager of the Manufacturing Investment Company's paper mills in Maine. In 1893 he moved to New York and began business as a consulting engineer.

O ver a century after Frederick Taylor's work began, his influence on how we work and how we perceive work remains undeniably significant. Robert Waterman, co-author of *In Search of Excellence*, believes that most managers remain Taylorists at heart.

Taylor was the instigator of what became known as 'Scientific Management' – and *The Principles of Scientific Management* is its bible. Scientific management emerged from Taylor's work at the Midvale Steel Works, where he was chief engineer. Taylor's 'science' came from the minute examination of individual tasks. Having identified every single movement and action involved in doing something, Taylor could determine the optimum time required to complete a task. Armed with this information, the manager could determine whether a person was doing the job well. 'In its essence, scientific management involves a complete mental revolution on the part of the working man engaged in any particular establishment or industry – a complete mental revolution on the part of these men as to their duties toward their work, toward their fellow men, and toward their employees,' Taylor writes.

'At the time Taylor began his work, business management as a discrete and identifiable activity had attracted little attention,' observed the British champion of scientific management, Lyndall Urwick (1956). 'It was usually regarded as incidental to, and flowing from knowledge-of-acquaintance-with, a particular branch of manufacturing, the technical know-how of making sausages or steel or shirts . . . The idea that a man needed any training or formal instruction to become a competent manager had not occurred to anyone.'

Scientific management had an effect throughout the world. A Japanese engineer translated *The Principles of Scientific Management* (in Japan it became *Secrets for Eliminating Futile Work and Increasing Production*). In Japan it was a bestseller – a foretaste of the Japanese willingness to embrace the latest Western thinking. Taylor even numbered Lenin among his admirers – 'We should try out every scientific and progressive suggestion in the Taylor system,' noted the Communist leader.

The legacy of Taylor's work remains in companies with a predilection to emphasize quantity over quality and was enthusiastically taken up by Henry Ford in the development of mass production techniques.

While Taylor's concepts are now usually regarded in a negative light, the originality of his insights and their importance are in little doubt. 'Few people had ever looked at human work systematically until Frederick W. Taylor started to do so around 1885. Work was taken for granted and it is an axiom that one never sees what one takes for granted. Scientific Management was thus one of the great liberating, pioneering insights,' observes Peter Drucker in *The Practice of Management*.

Drucker goes on to identify two fundamental flaws in scientific management. First, it denies integration – 'The first of these blind spots is the belief that because we must analyze work into its simplest constituent motions we must also organize it as a series of individual motions, each if possible carried out by an individual worker' – and second that it divorces planning from doing.

The most obvious consequence of scientific management is a dehumanizing reliance on measurement. Taylor envisaged no room for individual initiative or imagination. People were labor, mechanically accomplishing a particular task. Robert McNamara has reflected on the end result: 'The system disenfranchised those who were so important in the early stages of American manufacturing, the foremen and plant managers. Instead of being creators and innovators, as in an earlier era, now they depended on meeting production quotas. They lost any stake in stopping the line and fixing problems as they occurred; they lost any stake in innovation or change.'[1]

The plus side of Taylor's work has been outlined by Tom Peters, an unlikely ally. 'In his own fashion, time-and-motion man Frederick Taylor increased human freedom. His schemes for objectively determining "best practices" for every imaginable job helped free front-line workers from the capricious discipline of unscientific, turn-of-the-century foremen.' Indeed, the fact that Taylor's anticipated revolution was two-sided can be forgotten. 'It involves the equally complete mental revolution on the part of those on the management's side – the foremen, the superintendent, the owner of the business, the board of directors – a complete mental revolution on their part as to their duties toward their fellow workers in the management, toward their workmen, and toward all of their daily problems. And without this complete mental revolution on both sides scientific management does not exist.'

The Principles of Scientific Management stands now as a historical artifact. The ideas contained in it, however, live on.

Notes

1 Quoted in Shapley, Deborah, *Promise and Power: The Life and Times of Robert McNamara*, Little, Brown, Boston, 1993.

ALVIN TOFFLER

The Third Wave

1980

Hamel on Toffler

"The post-industrial society is here! And Alvin Toffler saw it coming in 1980. I don't think there's any such thing as a futurist, only people who have more finely tuned antennae, or who are better at understanding the medium-term implications of things that are already changing around them. One of the challenges for anyone reading Toffler, or any other seer, is that there is no proprietary data about the future – your competitors read Toffler, Naisbitt and Negraponte too! The real challenge is to build proprietary foresight out of public data! Good luck!"

Alvin Toffler

Alvin Toffler is a bestselling futurologist. His most significant books are *Future Shock*, *The Third Wave*, and *Power Shift*. Toffler was a Washington correspondent and an Associate Editor of *Fortune* before spending time as a Visiting Professor at Cornell University, a Visiting Scholar at the Russell Sage Foundation and teaching at the New School for Social Research.

lvin Toffler's *The Third Wave* ushers in the new technological era and bids farewell to the Second Wave of industrialization. 'Old ways of thinking, old formulas, dogmas, and ideologies, no matter how cherished or how useful in the past, no longer fit the facts,' Toffler writes. 'The world that is fast emerging from the clash of new values and technologies, new geopolitical relationships, new lifestyles and modes of communication, demands wholly new ideas and analogies, classifications and concepts.'

The Third Wave is the super-industrial society – 'the death of industrialism and the rise of a new civilization' – which was preceded by industrialization and the First Wave, the agricultural phase of civilization's development.

The Third Wave is characterized by mass customization rather than mass production. 'The essence of Second Wave manufacture was the long "run" of millions of identical standardized products. By contrast, the essence of Third Wave manufacture is the short run of partially or completely customized products,' writes Toffler. This notion of mass customization has since been picked up by a wide variety of thinkers and, in some areas, is already in existence.

Whereas the Second Wave strictly separated consumer and producer, Toffler predicts the Third Wave will see the two become almost indistinguishable, as the consumer becomes involved in the actual process of production, expressing choices and preferences. 'The customer will become so integrated into the production process that we will find it more and more difficult to tell just who is actually the consumer and who the producer,' says Toffler. He goes on to invent a word to describe this new being: the prosumer.

What is startling about *The Third Wave* is that it was written so recently and yet the technological leaps made since its publication have been so immense. Toffler, for example, has to explain what a word processor is – and mentions its alternative labels, 'the smart typewriter' or 'text editor'. He envisages the office of the future: 'The ultimate beauty of the electronic office lies not merely in the steps saved by a secretary in typing and correcting letters. The automated office can file them in the form of electronic bits on tape or disc. It can (or soon will) pass them through an electronic dictionary that will automatically correct their spelling errors. With the machines hooked up to one another and to the phone lines, the secretary can instantly transmit the letter to its recipient's printer or screen.' In 1980 to the vast majority of Toffler's readers this read like science fiction. In 1996 it is reality to the vast majority of people in the industrialized world (or de-industrialized world, according to Toffler's perspective).

Toffler predicts the demise of the nine to five working day. 'Machine synchronization shackled the human to the machine's capabilities and imprisoned all of social life in a common frame. It did so in capitalist and socialist countries alike. Now, as machine synchronization grows more precise, humans, instead of being imprisoned, are progressively freed,' says Toffler. They are freed into more flexible ways of working whether it is flexitime or working at home.

Toffler is not, however, a hopeless utopian. While the futurists of the early 1970s predicted a leisure age which failed to materialize, Toffler is aware of the broader ramifications of technology: 'The image of the office of the future is too neat, too smooth, too disembodied to be real. Reality is always messy. But it is clear that we are rapidly on our way, and even a partial shift towards the electronic office will be enough to trigger an eruption of social, psychological, and economic consequences. The coming word-quake means more than just new machines. It promises to restructure all the human relationships and roles in the office as well.'

It is this awareness of the broader impact of technological change which marks *The Third Wave*. Other studies of the future of our working lives tend to plunge head first into celebrations of the miracles of technology with little attempt to understand the human implications. To Toffler, the human side of change is all important. The Third Wave, he anticipates, 'will produce anxiety and conflict as well as reorganization, restructuring, and – for some – rebirth into new careers and opportunities. The new systems will challenge all the old executive turfs, the hierarchies, the sexual role divisions, the departmental barriers of the past'. Through reengineering, downsizing, empowerment and the management of diversity, as well as a host of other trends, the new systems described by Toffler can be seen to be in place today.

Toffler also accurately predicts the growth of regionalism and the profusion of local media. This, in another of Toffler's ungainly phrases, is the 'de-massifying' of our culture.

The immense implications for organizations are explored by Toffler. 'Instead of clinging to a sharply specialized economic function, the corporation, prodded by criticism, legislation, and its own concerned executives, is becoming a multipurpose institution,' says Toffler. The organization is being driven to redefinition through five forces:

1 **Changes in the physical environment**
   Companies are having to undertake greater responsibility for the effect of their operations on the environment.

2 **Changes in the 'line-up of social forces'**
   The actions of companies now have greater impact with those of other organizations such as schools, universities, civil groups and political lobbies.

3 **Changes in the role of information**
   'As information becomes central to production, as "information managers" proliferate in industry, the corporation, by necessity, impacts on the informational environment exactly as it impacts on the physical and social environment,' writes Toffler.

4 **Changes in government organization**
   The profusion of government bodies means that the

business and political worlds interact to a far greater degree than ever before.

5 **Changes in morality**
The ethics and values of organizations are becoming more closely linked to those of society. 'Behavior once accepted as normal is suddenly reinterpreted as corrupt, immoral or scandalous,' says Toffler. 'The corporation is increasingly seen as a producer of moral effects.'

The organization of the future, he envisages, will be concerned with ecological, moral, political, racial, sexual and social problems, as well as traditional commercial ones. Interestingly, it is here that Toffler's picture of the future has largely failed to become reality. While the ways in which work is structured in organizations and the jobs of individuals have been radically altered, in many cases revolutionized, the organization has moved far more slowly.

The Third Wave is far reaching and goes well beyond the impact of the emerging civilization on work and organizations. It has proved a highly accurate picture of a future which has largely arrived. Its ideas, such as the rise of homeworking, have since been developed by others, most notably by Charles Handy.

46

ROBERT TOWNSEND

Up the Organization

1970

Hamel on Townsend

"Irreverence, impiety, and non-conformity are essential to organizational vitality. They were also the ingredients that made *Up the Organization* essential reading for corporate iconoclasts of the 1970s. This is *Liberation Management* two and a half decades before people knew they needed to be liberated. The real question is, why do these books come along once every twenty or so years? We really are taking ourselves too seriously!"

Robert Townsend

Born in 1920, **Robert Townsend** was President of Avis until it was absorbed into the ITT empire. He is the author of *Up the Organization* and its sequel *Further Up the Organization*.

T he canon of management literature is not noted for its humor. Academic rigor is more highly prized than witty one-liners. And yet, every generation has produced a humorous bestseller debunking managerial mythology and the high-minded seriousness of the theorists. In the fifties there was *Parkinson's Law* and at the end of the sixties, Robert Townsend's *Up the Organization* (sub-titled 'How to stop the corporation from stifling people and strangling profits'). Robert Heller called the book 'the first pop bestseller on business management' which 'owed much of its success to Townsend's derisive title'.

The tone of *Up the Organization* is set from the start, in a memorandum on how to use the book. 'In the average company the boys in the mailroom, the president, the vice-presidents, and the girls in the steno pool have three things in common: they are docile, they are bored, and they are dull,' observes Townsend. 'Trapped in the pigeonholes of organization charts, they've been made slaves to the rules of private and public hierarchies that run mindlessly on and on because nobody can change them.'

Townsend then travels through the modern organization from A to Z. Townsend is, by turn, playful, indignant, critical and practical. His greatest vehemence is reserved for Harvard Business School – 'Don't hire Harvard Business School graduates,' he advises. 'This elite, in my opinion, is missing some pretty fundamental requirements for success: humility; respect for people on the firing line; deep understanding of the nature of the business and the kind of people who can enjoy themselves making it prosper; respect from way down the line; a demonstrated record of guts, industry, loyalty down, judgment, fairness, and honesty under pressure.'

More useful, if still obtuse, is Townsend's observation that 'top management (the board of directors) is supposed to be a tree full of owls – hooting when management heads into the wrong part of the forest. I'm still unpersuaded they even know where the forest is.'

There is a great deal of good sense buried in *Up the Organization*. Townsend has, for example, no time for the adornments of executive office and his list of 'no-nos' includes: reserved parking spaces; special-quality stationery for the boss and his elite; muzak; bells and buzzers; company shrinks; outside directorships and trusteeships for the chief executive ('Give up all those non-jobs. You can't even run your own company, dummy'); and the company plane. He is, in fact, preaching a brand of empowerment and participation which was 20 years ahead of its time.

'There's nothing fundamentally wrong with our country except that the leaders of all our major organizations are operating on the wrong assumptions,' Townsend writes. 'We're in this mess because for the last two hundred years we've been using the Catholic Church and Caesar's legions as our patterns for creating organizations, And until the last forty or fifty years it made sense. The average churchgoer, soldier, and factory worker was uneducated and dependent on orders from above. And authority carried considerable weight because disobedience brought the death penalty or its equivalent.'

Up the Organization is a child of its times – irreverent and humorous, questioning the accepted behavior of corporate society. Given that nearly 30 years have passed since its publication, it still retains its freshness and originality, and its insights into the blind deficiencies of too many organizations remain sadly apt.

47

FONS TROMPENAARS

Riding the Waves of Culture

1993

Hamel on Trompenaars

"So Americans will never understand 'foreign' cultures . . . Funny how American companies are out-competing their European competitors in Asia and Latin America. Name any region of the world that looks to Europe for its managerial inspiration. (Oh wait, sorry, I'm not supposed to be parochial!) Where I agree with Trompenaars is that the future belongs to the cosmopolitans."

Fons Trompenaars

Born in 1952, **Fons Trompenaars** is also co-author (with Charles Hampden-Turner) of *The Seven Cultures of Capitalism* (1994). Trompenaars' reputation is built on his work on the cultural aspects of modern management. The roots of this interest, he attributes to being brought up by a French mother and Dutch father. He studied at Wharton in the US and is now managing director of the Center for International Business Studies in Amstelveen in the Netherlands.

Management in a global environment is increasingly affected by cultural differences,' says Fons Trompenaars His *Riding the Waves of Culture* is an examination of the cultural imponderables faced by managers in the global village. 'Basic to understanding other cultures is the awareness that culture is a series of rules and methods that a society has evolved to deal with the recurring problems it faces,' writes Trompenaars. 'They have become so basic that, like breathing, we no longer think about how we approach or resolve them. Every country and every organization faces dilemmas in relationships with people; dilemmas in relationship to time; and dilemmas in relations between people and the natural environment. Culture is the way in which people resolve dilemmas emerging from universal problems.' *Riding the Waves of Culture* is based on meticulous quantitative research, and over 900 seminars presented in 18 countries. (Trompenaars' 15 years of research has now covered 15,000 people from 50 countries.)

Trompenaars is dismissive of the American managerial model – 'It is my belief that you can never understand other cultures ... I started wondering if any of the American management techniques I was brainwashed with in eight years of the best business education money could buy would apply in the Netherlands, where I came from, or indeed in the rest of the world.' The answer he provides is simply that they do not.

'The international manager needs to go beyond awareness of cultural differences,' Trompenaars writes. 'He or she needs to respect these differences and take advantage of diversity through reconciling cross-cultural dilemmas. The international manager reconciles cultural dilemmas.' Trompenaars' emphasis is not on the emotionally laden area of diversity but on how culture affects our behavior and how different cultures interact.

Trompenaars' findings are presented by way of seven

chapters examining the basic premises that make up a culture. He presents a number of fundamentally different cultural perspectives while acknowledging that within a country attachment to any given cultural trait varies widely.

The first of these is the conflict between what Trompenaars labels the 'universalist' and the 'particularist'. Universalists (including Americans, Canadians, Australians and the Swiss) advocate 'one best way', a set of rules that applies in any setting. Particularists (South Koreans, Chinese and Malaysians) focus on the peculiar nature of any given situation.

Trompenaars examines the extremes by way of archetypal situations. In the universalist-particularist conflict, he presents the following dilemma: You are in a car with a close friend who has an accident in which a third party is injured. You are the only witness, and he asks you to falsely testify about his driving speed. In such a situation, universalists won't lie for their friend while particularists will. The difference becomes even more pronounced if the injury is severe. The universalist becomes even more adherent to the rules while the particularist's sense of obligation grows. (In this example, 74 percent of South Koreans would assist their friend and lie, compared to just five percent of Americans.)

Such results allow Trompenaars to provide advice on how business dealings between the two parties might work. Universalists doing business with particularists should, for example, 'be prepared for meandering or irrelevancies that do not seem to be going anywhere'; moreover, we should not 'take get to know you chatter as small talk'. It is important to particularists. Particularists doing business with universalists should 'be prepared for rational and 'professional arguments and presentations'.

Then there is the 'collectivist' (group oriented) versus 'individualist' frame of mind. The Unites States again falls into the extremist category as emphasizing the individual before the group. Countries such as Egypt and France are at the other end. Individualists working with collectivists must tolerate 'time taken to ... consult' and negotiators who 'can only agree tentatively and may withdraw (an offer) after consulting with superiors'.

The difference between those who show their feelings (such as Italians) and those who hide them (such as the Japanese) is also profound. Other distinctions include how we accord status (through achievement rather than through ascription – based on family, age, etc.); and how we manage time (past versus future orientation).

The cultural imponderables and wide range of basic differences in how different cultures perceive the world provides a daunting picture of the world ridden with potential pitfalls. 'We need a certain amount of humility and a sense of humor to discover cultures other than our own; a readiness to enter a room in the dark and stumble over unfamiliar furniture until the pain in our shins reminds us of where things are,' he writes.

In the end, says Trompenaars, the only positive route forward is through reconciliation. 'Our hypothesis is that those societies that can reconcile better are better at creating wealth,' he says.[1] Whether this will be borne out by the future experience of transnational organizations will continue to be discussed. What can be said is that the cultural aspects of managing internationally are likely to gain in importance as the full force of globalization affects industries and individuals.

Notes

1 Quoted in Houlder, V., 'Interview with Fons Trompenaars', *Financial Times*, 26 July, 1996.

48

SUN TZU

The Art of War

500 BC

Hamel on Sun Tzu

"Strategy didn't start with Igor Ansoff, neither did it start with Machiavelli. It probably didn't even start with Sun Tzu. Strategy is as old as human conflict – and if the stakes are high in business, they're rather higher in the military sphere. In fact, one of the best strategy books I've ever read is *Military Misfortune* by two professors of military strategy at America's naval college."

Sun Tzu

The authorship of *The Art of War* remains, perhaps understandably, clouded in mystery. It may have been written by **Sun Wu,** a military general who was alive around 500 BC. His book is reputed to have led to a meeting between Sun Wu and King Ho-lü of Wu. Sun Wu, not having a flip chart available, argued his case for military discipline by decapitating two of the King's concubines. The book's actual title is *Sun Tzu Ping Fa* which can be literally translated as 'The military method of venerable Mr. Sun'.

M ilitary examples and imagery have played an important role in the development of management thinking. Even now, military role models – whether they are Colin Powell or Norman Schwarzkopf – are keenly seized upon by executives. The military, with its elements of strategy and leadership, is alluring and the link between the military and business worlds has existed since time immemorial. Books as diverse as Carl Von Clausewitz's *On War* (1908), B.H. Liddell-Hart's *Strategy* (1967) and Miyamoto Mushashi's *A Book of Five Rings* (1974) have explored the link. Its starting point, as far as it is possible to discern, is Sun Tzu's *The Art of War* written 2,500 years ago.

Generally, the attraction of the military analogy is that it is clear who your enemy is. When your enemy is clear, the world appears clearer if you are a military general or a managing director. Sun Tzu's *The Art of War* is usually interpreted in such terms, as an aggressive counterpoint to the confusion of mere theory. In fact, *The Art of War* is more sophisticated than that. Why destroy when you can win by stealth and cunning? 'A sovereign should not start a war out of anger, nor should a general give battle out of rage. For while anger can revert to happiness and rage to delight, a nation that has been destroyed cannot be restored, nor can the dead be brought back to life,' writes Sun Tzu. 'To subdue the enemy's forces without fighting is the summit of skill. The best approach is to attack the other side's strategy; next best is to attack his alliances; next best is to attack his soldiers; the worst is to attack cities.'

Sun Tzu also has sound advice on knowing your markets. 'Advance knowledge cannot be gained from ghosts and spirits ... but must be obtained from people who know the enemy situation.'

Elsewhere, Sun Tzu lapses into Confucian analogies which would appear to be anathema to hardheaded modern executives. Often, however, they appear to find them reassuring. 'For the shape of an army is like that of water,' says Sun Tzu. 'The shape of water is to avoid heights and flow towards low places; the shape of the army is to avoid strength and to strike at weakness. Water flows in accordance with the ground; an army achieves victory in accordance with the enemy.'

The Art of War is best known as the origin of the concept of strategy, one that has been through a great many re-interpretations in the intervening 2500 years. Here, there is no room for sentiment or distraction: 'Deploy forces to defend the strategic points; exercise vigilance in preparation, do not be indolent. Deeply investigate the true situation, secretly await their laxity. Wait until they leave their strongholds, then seize what they love.'

49

THOMAS WATSON JR.

A Business and Its Beliefs: The Ideas that Helped Build IBM

1963

Hamel on Watson Jr.

"Never change your basic beliefs, Watson argued. He may be right. But the dividing line between beliefs and dogmas is a fine one. A deep set of beliefs can be the essential pivot around which the company changes and adapts; or, if endlessly elaborated, overly codified, and solemnly worshipped, the manacles that shackle a company to the past."

Thomas Watson Jr.
(1914–1993)

The son of the legendary founder of IBM, Thomas Watson Sr. **Thomas Watson Jr.** attended Brown University and served in the Air Corps during World War Two. He joined IBM in 1946 and worked as a salesman. He became chief executive in 1956 and retired in 1970. He was then US ambassador in Moscow until 1980.

Though always in the shadow of his father, under Watson IBM was propelled to the forefront of the technological revolution. He invested heavily in the development of System/360 which formed the basis of the company's success in the 1970s and 1980s. As well as *A Business and Its Beliefs*, Watson also wrote an autobiography *Father, Son & Co* (1990).

T homas Watson's *A Business and Its Beliefs: The Ideas that Helped Build IBM* is a statement of business philosophy, an extended mission statement for the corporate giant. Though it was published in the same year as Alfred P. Sloan's *My Years with General Motors* it could not be more different. While Sloan sidelines people, Watson celebrates their potential; while Sloan espouses systems and structures, Watson talks of values.

Behind *A Business and Its Beliefs*, stands the more Sloan-like, sober figure of Thomas Watson Sr. (1874–1956). Watson Senior was the creator of IBM – something which his son certainly never forgot. ('The secret I learned early on from my father was to run scared and never think I had made it,' he said.)

IBM's origins lay in the Computing-Tabulating-Recording Company which Watson Sr. joined in 1914. Under his leadership the company's revenues doubled from $4.2 million to $8.3 million by 1917. Initially making everything from butcher's scales to meat slicers, its activities gradually concentrated on tabulating machines which processed information mechanically on punched cards. Watson, however, had grander aspirations. 'Father came home from work, gave mother a hug, and proudly announced that the Computing-Tabulating-Recording Company, henceforth would be known by the grand name International Business Machines,' recalled Watson Jr. in his autobiography. 'I stood in the doorway of the living room thinking, "That little outfit?" Dad must have had in mind the IBM of the future. The one he actually ran was still full of cigar-chomping guys selling coffee grinders and butcher scales.'

IBM's development was helped by the 1937 Wages-Hours Act which required US companies to record hours worked and wages paid. The existing machines could not cope and Watson instigated work on a solution. In 1944 the Mark 1 was launched, followed by the Selective Sequence Electronic Calculator in 1947. By then IBM's revenues were

$119 million and it was set to make the great leap forward to become the world's largest computer company.

Thomas Watson Jr. took on a hugely successful company with a strong corporate culture built around salesmanship and service. In *Liberation Management* Tom Peters notes that Thomas Watson Sr. 'emphasized people and service – obsessively. IBM was a service star in an era of malperforming machines'.

In *A Business and Its Beliefs*, Thomas Watson Jr. codifies and clarifies what IBM stands for. Central to this are the company's central beliefs (or what would now be called core values). 'I believe the real difference between success and failure in a corporation can very often be traced to the question of how well the organization brings out the great energies and talents of its people. What does it do to help these people find common cause with each other?' writes Watson. 'And how can it sustain this common cause and sense of direction through the many changes which take place from one generation to another?'

The answer, says Watson, comes through 'a sound set of beliefs, on which it premises all its policies and actions. Next, I believe that the most important single factor in corporate success is faithful adherence to those beliefs ... beliefs must always come before policies, practices, and goals. The latter must always be altered if they are seen to violate fundamental beliefs.'

Beliefs, says Watson, never change. Change everything else, but never the basic truths on which the company is based – 'If an organization is to meet the challenges of a changing world, it must be prepared to change everything about itself except beliefs as it moves through corporate life ... The only sacred cow in an organization should be its basic philosophy of doing business.'

In *A Business and Its Beliefs* Watson Jr. tellingly observes: 'The beliefs that mold great organizations frequently grow out of the character, the experience and the convictions of a single person.' In IBM's case that person was Thomas Watson Senior. The Watsons created a corporate culture which lasted. IBM – 'Big Blue' – became the archetypal modern corporation and its managers the ultimate stereotype – with their regulation somber suits, white shirts, plain ties, zeal for selling and company song. Beneath this, however, lay a belief in competing vigorously and providing quality service. Later, competitors complained that IBM's sheer size won it orders. This was only partly true. Its size masked a deeper commitment to managing customer accounts, providing service, building relationships and to the values laid out by Watson in *A Business and Its Beliefs*.

MAX WEBER

The Theory of Social and Economic Organization

1947

Hamel on Weber

"Every organization wrestles with two conflicting needs: the need to optimize in the name of economic efficiency, and the need to experiment in the name of growth and renewal. Authoritarian bureaucracies, of the sort that re-built the Japanese economy after the war, serve well the goal of optimization – while there *is* experimentation here, it is tightly constrained. Anarchical networks, of the sort that predominate in Italy's fashion industry, allow for unfettered experimentation, but are always vulnerable to more disciplined competitors. Weber staked out one side of the argument; Tom Peters the other. As always, what is required is a synthesis."

Max Weber (1864-1920)

Max Weber was a multi-talented German who was ill-served by the notion that he was simply the father of bureaucracy. After studying legal and economic history, Weber was a Professor at the University of Freiburg and later at the University of Heidelberg.

He studied the sociology of religion and in this area he produced his best known work *The Protestant Work Ethic and the Spirit of Capitalism*. In political sociology he examined the relationship between social and economic organizations.

Towards the end of his life, Weber developed his political interests and was on the committee which drafted the constitution of the Weimar Republic in 1918.

I n terms of management theorizing Max Weber is something of a *bête noir*, the sociological twin of Frederick Taylor. Weber 'pooh-poohed charismatic leadership and doted on bureaucracy; its rule-driven, impersonal form, he said, was the only way to assure long-term survival' observed Peters and Waterman in *In Search of Excellence*.

Weber's *The Theory of Social and Economic Organization* argues that the most efficient form of organization resembles a machine. It is characterized by strict rules, controls and hierarchies and driven by bureaucracy. This, Weber terms, the 'rational-legal model'. At the opposite extreme are the 'charismatic' model and the 'traditional' model where things are done as they always have been such as in family firms in which power is passed down from one generation to the next.

'Experience tends universally to show that the purely bureaucratic type of administrative organization – that is, the monocratic variety of bureaucracy – is, from a purely technical point of view, capable of attaining the highest degree of efficiency and is in this sense formally the most rational known means of carrying our imperative control over human beings,' Weber writes. 'It is superior to any other form in precision, in stability, in the stringency of its discipline, and in its reliability. It thus makes possible a particularly high degree of calculability of results for the heads of the organization and for those acting in relation to it. It is finally superior both in intensive efficiency and in the scope of its operations and is formally capable of application to all kinds of administrative tasks.'

In *The Theory of Social and Economic Organization* Weber outlines the 'structure of authority' around seven points:

1 A continuous organization of official functions bound by rules.
2 A specified sphere of competence.
3 The organization of offices follows the principle of hierarchy.

4 The rules which regulate the conduct of an office may be technical rules or norms. In both cases, if their application is to be fully traditional, specialized training is necessary.
5 In the rational type it is a matter of principle that the members of the administrative staff should be completely separated from the ownership of the means of production or administration.
6 n the rational type case, there is also a complete absence of appropriation of his official position by the incumbent.
7 Administrative acts, decisions and rules are formulated and recorded in writing, even in cases where oral discussion is the rule or is even mandatory.

While it would be easy to dismiss Weber as an authoritarian voice from another era, this would be unfair. He was, by turns, perplexed and concerned about the implications of his rational bureaucratic model for humanity. His net was, in fact, far wider. At its heart was the search for some understanding of the relationship between science, politics, knowledge and action.

Though he dismissed the charismatic model as a long-term solution, he was the first to acknowledge its existence and to examine its ramifications. History bears Weber out – an organization built around a single charismatic figure is unsustainable in the long-term.

The bureaucratic world mapped out by Weber to some extent came to pass. While it is easy to criticize the dehumanizing impact of such overpowering bureaucracies, their role in developing businesses in the early part of the twentieth century cannot be underestimated.

APPENDIX

No list can ever be complete or fully comprehensive. Among the other books considered for *The Ultimate Business Library* were the following fifty.

1
Louis Allen
Professional Management: new concepts and proven practices
1973

Following two decades of research, in *Professional Management* Allen puts forward four functions of management based on a belief that managers think and act rationally – planning, organizing, leading and controlling. These are then further divided into 19 management activities.

2
Chris Argyris
Personality and Organization
1957

In this classic work of behavioral science, Argyris argues that organizations depend fundamentally on people. The book is concerned with how personal development is and can be related to work. The problem, Argyris believes, in many organizations is that the organization itself stands in the way of people fulfilling their potential. The task for the organization is to make sure that people's motivation and potential are fulfilled and well-directed.

3
Charles Babbage
On the Economy of Machines and Manufactures
1832

Charles Babbage (1792–1871) produced perhaps the first business bestseller in his study of British factories. His work and observations are only a step away from Frederick Taylor's at the end of the nineteenth century (though there is no evidence that Taylor read Babbage). 'It is of great importance to know the precise expenses of every process as well as of the wear and tear of machinery which is due to it,' wrote Babbage. Taylor went on to utilize the same enthusiasm for measurement to human performance.

4
Warren Bennis
The Temporary Society
1968

A child of the sixties, *The Temporary Society* marked Bennis' highest point as a futurologist and social commentator. In it he envisages organizations as adhocracies – roughly the direct opposite of bureaucracies – freed from the shackles of hierarchy and meaningless paperwork. Alvin Toffler late used the phrase, and made it famous, in *Future Shock*.

5
Robert Blake & Jane Mouton
The Managerial Grid
1964

The Managerial Grid method of designating various styles of leadership shows how a leader can simultaneously maximize both production and people-oriented methods of management. It identifies four extremes of management style and measures them on the two dimensions of production and people.

6
Kenneth Blanchard & Spencer Johnson
The One Minute Manager
1982

A much-ridiculed concept and book, yet it proved to be a bestseller, launching a host of imitators and generating the self-help movement of which Stephen Covey is the most notable exponent. Blanchard and Johnson's hope is that the book's readers 'will enjoy healthier, happier and more productive lives'.

7
Edward de Bono
The Use of Lateral Thinking
1967

Edward De Bono (born 1933) has made a career from the success of this single book. Lateral thinking is concerned with thinking in a discontinuous way, turning ideas on their head.

8
Richard Boyatzis
The Competent Manager:
a model for effective performance
1982

The study behind Boyatzis' book involved over 2,000 managers who held 41 different jobs in 12 different public and private organizations. The result was a generic model of managerial competencies applicable in different contexts and organization types. The resulting model comprises 12 competencies in six clusters.

9
E.F.L. Brech (editor)
The Principles and Practice of Management
1953

Brech was a British apostle of the early management theorists and in *The Principles and Practice of Management* gathers together a comprehensive history of scientific management and early pioneers of management thinking.

10
Tom Burns & G.M. Stalker
The Management of Innovation
1961

Warren Bennis has described *The Management of Innovation* as a 'major classic'. The sociologist, Burns, and psychologist, Stalker, identified the 'organic' organization characterized by networks, shared vision and values, and teamworking, echoing many contemporary theorists.

11
Jan Carlzon
Moments of Truth
1987

The Scandinavian Airline chief, Carlzon, recorded his approach to management and customer care in *Moments of Truth*, so-called because when the customer meets a representative of the company it is, says Carlzon, a moment of truth. Entitled *Riv Pyramiderna!* ('flatten the Pyramids') in Swedish, it recounts how Carlzon turned the loss-making airline into airline of the year.

12
James Collins & Jerry Porras
Built to Last: Successful habits of visionary companies
1995

A study of 18 companies which have achieved long-term success – average age over 90. Their success is built on charismatic leadership which creates a dynamic culture built around core sustainable values.

13
Philip Crosby
Quality is Free
1979

Philip Crosby's quality gospel was populist and popular. Proclaiming that 'reducing the cost of quality is in fact an opportunity to increase profits without raising sales, buying new equipment, or hiring new people', Crosby proved a barnstorming evangelist in the early years of the quality resurgence.

14
Robert Cyert & James March
A Behavioral Theory of the Firm
1963

The duo from Pittsburgh's Carnegie-Mellon University explored the rationality of managerial decision making. Unlike some others, Cyert and March concluded that decisions were not always rational and advocated creative decision making. This, they said, could be achieved through experimentation, which they labeled 'the technology of foolishness'. In a far-sighted term, they believed organizations were a 'coalition of interests'.

15
Terence Deal & Allan Kennedy
Corporate Cultures:
The rites and rituals of corporate life
1982

Deal and Kennedy argue that strong cultures lead to strong businesses and believe cultures are driven by values, heroes, and roles and rituals.

16
Peter F. Drucker
Management: Tasks, Responsibilities, Practices
1974

Drucker poignantly and persuasively argues the case for management. 'Management is tasks. Management is discipline. But management is also people,' he writes. 'Every achievement of management is the achievement of a manager. Every failure is the failure of a manager. People manage, rather than "forces" or "facts". The vision, dedication and integrity of managers determine whether there is management or mismanagement.' This huge 1974 book serves as an updating of his 1954 classic, *The Practice of Management* (see Chapter 12).

17
Fred Fiedler & Martin Chemers
Leadership and Effective Management
1974

A theoretical study of the problems of leadership addressing three questions: how one becomes a leader, how leaders behave and what makes the leader effective. Developing from Situational Theory, contingency approaches attempt to elect situational variables which best indicate the most appropriate leadership style to suit the circumstances. Fred Fiedler, for example, found the critical factors of a leadership situation to be leader-member relations, task structure and the position power of the leader.

18
Charles Garfield
Peak Performers: The New Heroes in Business
1986

Garfield's study of *Peak Performers* provided impetus to the growing trend to examine the psychology of successful people. Garfield refers to the key skill of self-mastery – orchestrating and developing capabilities and seeking opportunities within organizations which further personal growth – and concludes that development must begin with the individual.

19
Harold Geneen and Alvin Moscow
Managing
1985

The archetypal bullish executive, Geneen transformed ITT into a massive corporate power. His tactics were simple: hard work and an apparently slavish devotion to figures – 'Putting deals together beats spending every day playing golf,' said Geneen. ITT rapidly disintegrated following Geneen's departure, but Managing provides a rare insight into a managerial type rarely discussed elsewhere.

20
Frank Gilbreth
Motion Study
1911

Gilbreth (1868–1924) and his wife Lilian (1878–1972) were innovative and entrepreneurial exponents of Scientific Management. They took Frederick Taylor's ideas forward through more intensive study of what worker's actually did. 'Eliminating unnecessary distances that workers' hands and arms must travel will eliminate miles of motions per man in a working day as compared with usual practice,' Gilbreth concludes.

21
Michael Goold and Andrew Campbell
Strategies and Styles
1987

In diversified companies the problems of providing a sense of focus are often immense. This book examines the role of the corporate center in such companies. Based on four years of research it argues the case for and the place of strategies and concludes there are three dominant styles: strategic planning, strategic control and financial control. The best style for a particular company depends on the nature of the business and its long-term strategic objectives.

22
Charles Handy
Understanding Organizations
1976

Handy's first book is a clearly written textbook on organizational theorists and theories. It clarified Handy's own perspectives on the subject, but also serves to clarify those of its readers. 'I would encourage anyone else to burn this book after reading it and start to write their own – it's the only way to really own the concepts,' says Handy.

23
Charles Handy
The Empty Raincoat
1994

Re-titled *The Age of Paradox* in the US, this bestseller develops many of the ideas first covered by Handy in *The Age of Unreason*. In *The Empty Raincoat* Handy champions the 'federal' organization, 'an old idea whose time may have come'. The federal organization allows units and divisions individual independence while preserving corporate unity. Through federalism Handy believes the modern company can bridge some of the paradoxes it continually faces – such as the need to be simultaneously global and local.

24
Robert Hayes & Stephen Wheelwright
Restoring Our Competitive Edge
1984

The Harvard duo were at the forefront of America's re-examination of its competitiveness in the early 1980s. Their book argues that well run factories throughout the world have similarities. It tackles the mythology of Japanese production techniques and argues the case for a competitive and practically implemented manufacturing strategy. Its origins may be seen in the famous 1981 *Harvard Business Review* article, 'Managing our way to economic decline', by Hayes and Bill Abernathy.

25
Paul Hersey
Situational Leadership
1984

Situational Theory views leadership as specific to a situation rather than a particular sort of personality. It is based round the plausible notion that different circumstances require different forms of leadership. Its champions include Paul Hersey and Kenneth Blanchard. Hersey's influential book, *Situational Leadership* remains a situationalist manifesto.

26
Elliott Jacques
A General Theory of Bureaucracy
1976

Jacques' theories emerged from an extensive research project with the Glacier Metal Company between 1948 and 1965. His novel conclusion was labeled the *time span of discretion* which contended that levels of management should be based on how long it was before their decisions could be checked, and that people should be paid in accordance with that time.

27
Rosabeth Moss Kanter
When Giants Learn to Dance
1989

Introduced the concept of the post-entrepreneurial firm which manages to combine the traditional strengths of a large organization with the flexible speed of a smaller organization.

28
John Kotter
A Force for Change
1990

Kotter argues that 'leadership produces change. That is its primary function'. He goes on to examine the role of leadership in producing organizational change. He says that leadership is characterized by establishing direction; aligning people; motivating and inspiring; and producing change. In contrast management is concerned with planning and budgeting; organizing and staffing; controlling and problem solving; and produces a degree of predictability and order.

29
Charles Kepner and Benjamin Tregoe
The Rational Manager
1965

'The capacity to reason systematically is unquestionably a basic necessity for any manger,' argue Kepner and Tregoe offering 'a systematic approach to problem solving and decision making'. The techniques detailed in *The Rational Manager* have laid the basis for the duo's consultancy firm's enduring success and were updated in *The New Rational Manager*.

30
Rensis Likert
New Patterns of Management
1961

Likert (1903–81) developed four types – systems 1 to 4 – of management style. The first is exploitative and authoritarian; the second, 'benevolent autocracy'; the thrid, 'consultative' and the fourth 'participative'. The latter was seen by Likert as the best option – both in a business and a personal sense. He also proposed System 5 in which there was no formal authority.

31
Konosuke Matsushita
Quest for Prosperity:
The Life of a Japanese Industrialist
1988

Inspired by Henry Ford, Matsushita (1894–1989) founded a company which grew to be the largest consumer electronics company in the world. Though he left school aged nine, Matsushita became the benevolent patriarch of the Japanese business world. He pioneered Japanese management and its social conscience, customer service and just-in-time philosophy. Matsushita later shared some of his insights with Richard Pascale.

32
Elton Mayo
The Human Problems of an Industrial Civilization
1933

Elton Mayo (1880–1949) is best known, and judged, by his research rather than his published works. His role in the Hawthorne Studies at Western Electric in 1927–32 was critical in the development of the human relations school of thinkers which later emerged. His championing of team-working, informal organization and communication is only now being recognized.

33
James Mooney & Alan Reiley
Onward Industry
1931

Mooney and Reilley's study of organizational principles was the first sytematic study of the organization along scientific lines.

34
Ann Morrison, Randall White & Ellen Van Velsor
Breaking the Glass Ceiling
1992

This book by academics then based at the Center for Creative Leadership established the term 'glass ceiling' in the human resources vocabulary. Based on a three-year study of female executives, it examines the factors which determine success or 'derailment' for women in the corporate environment.

35
John Naisbitt
Megatrends
1982

Naisbitt aticipates many of the tredns and business preoccupations of the last decade in this bestseller. He beckons in the information age, characterized by self-reliance and lack of conventional hierarchies. 'We are exploding into a freewheeling multiple-option society,' Naisbitt predicts.

36
Kenichi Ohmae
Triad Power:
The Coming Shape of Global Competition
1985

The Triad described by Ohmae consists of the United States, Japan and the Pacific, and Europe. Ohmae suggests that the route to global competitivenes is to establish a presence in each area of the Triad which has deep roots in the local culture. Also, companies must utilize the three Cs of commitment, creativity and competitiveness.

37
William Ouchi
Theory Z
1981

Ouchi's book was a major contributor to the fascination in the 1980s, and later, with Japanese management. Ouchi, sub-titled the book, 'The Japanese challenge', and took as his starting point Douglas McGregor's unfinished contemplation of the theory beyond Theories X and Y. In the Japanese practices of life-time employment and company values, Ouchi found a rich source of material echoing many of the ideas initially contemplated by McGregor.

38
David Packard
The HP Way:
How Bill Hewlett and I Built Our Company
1995

With a mere $538 and a rented garage in Palo Alto, Hewlett and Packard created one of the most successful corporations in the world. Their secret, says Packard, lies in the simplicity of their methods.

39
Laurence Peter & Raymond Hull
The Peter Principle
1969

Hilarious, but true, the Peter Principle is simply that 'In a hierarchy, every employee tends to rise to his own level of incompetence'. It includes an essential glossary which includes 'tabulatory gaintism: obsession with large size desks'.

40
Tom Peters
Thriving on Chaos
1987

Thriving on Chaos launched the second phase of Peters' career. After the success of *In Search of Excellence* and the story-filled *A Passion for Excellence*, Peters expands his horizons. He also acknowledges the deficiencies of his previous two books, proclaiming 'Excellence RIP'.

41
Reg Revans
Action Learning
1979

Unsung and unheralded, the UK's Reg Revans is the founder and long-time champion of action learning. As theories go action learning is simple, deceptively so. It is concerned with learning to learn by doing, a process for which Revans created a simple equation – $L = P + Q$ – learning occurs through a combination of programed knowledge (P) and the ability to ask insightful questions (Q). *Action Learning* is a huge, largely unacknowledged, book – Revans ended up buying most of the copies.

42
Richard Schonberger
Building a Chain of Customers
1990

Devloping from his earlier work, Schonberger suggests that each function in a business should be regarded as a customer. This, in effect, laid the foundation for what was to emerge as reengineering.

43
E. Fritz Schumacher
Small is Beautiful
1973

E. Fritz Schumacher (1911–77) advocated small-scale production working with nature and using 'intermediate technology'. Small is beautiful was an antidote to the prevailing
corporate mentality. It became a surprising bestseller though
it is only in the last five years that its ideas have begun to be
translated into reality – and then only partially.

44
Herbert Simon
Administrative Behavior
1947

'*Administrative Behavior* was written on the assumption that
decision-making processes hold the key to the understanding
of organizational phenomena,' says Simon who goes on to
explore the limits of rationality.

45
George Stalk & Thomas Hout
Competing Against Time
1990

Stalk and Hout of the Boston Consulting Group launched the
fashion for 'time-based competition' with this book. 'As time
is compressed, share increases,' is the basic and simple message.

46
Lyndall Urwick
Scientific Principles of Organization
1938

Lyndall Urwick was the British champion of management
thinking and education in the first half of the twentieth century. He was an eager proponent of Frederick Taylor's

Scientific Management and did much to publicize the theories of both Taylor and Henri Fayol. In *Scientific Principles of Organization* he develops and expands on the ideas of both of his inspirations.

47
William Whyte
The Organization Man
1956

If Arthur Miller's *Death of a Salesman* is the classic fifties drama portraying the sorrows of selling, William Whyte's *The Organization Man* is a less dramatic accompanying volume describing the mind-numbing mundanity of life shackled to the desk constrained by rigid corporate rules and hierarchy.

48
J.P. Womack, D.T. Jones & D. Roos
The Machine that Changed the World
1990

An introduction to the new industrial world where mass production has given way to mass customization, and the emphasis is on lean production. Uses the automobile industry as a historical and contemporary example of a sea-change in manufacturing.

49
Abraham Zaleznik
The Managerial Mystique:
Restoring Leadership in Business
1990

The differences – and similarities – between leadership and management have caused numerous debates and few conclusions. Zaleznik argues that we have 'a need for competent managers and a longing for great leaders' and analyzes the differences between the two which, in part, are as much a characteristic of etymology than anything else.

50
Shoshana Zuboff
In the Age of the Smart Machine
1988

Harvard's Zuboff proclaims that learning is the new source of competitive advantage and advises corporations to 'informate' – an unappetizing, but accurate, combination of inform and communicate. Though not a mainstream bestseller, Zuboff's book has proved influential.

BIBLIOGRAPHY

Andrews, K.R., 'Introduction to the Anniversary Edition', *The Functions of the Executive*, Harvard University Press, Cambridge, Mass, 1968.

Ansoff, H.I., *Corporate Strategy*, McGraw Hill, New York, 1965.

Ansoff, H.I., *Strategic Management*, Macmillan, London, 1979.

Ansoff, H.I., *Implanting Strategic Management*, Prentice Hall, London, 1984.

Ansoff, H.I., 'A profile of intellectual growth' in *Management Laureates*, JAI Press, London, 1994.

Ansoff, H.I., *New Corporate Strategy*, John Wiley, New York, 1989.

Argyris, C., *Personality and Organization*, Harper & Row, New York, 1957.

Argyris, C., *Understanding Organizational Behavior*, Dorsey Press, Homewood, Illinois, 1960.

Argyris, C., *Overcoming Organizational Defenses*, Allyn & Bacon, Boston, 1990.

Argyris, C. and Schon, D., *Organizational Learning: A Theory of Action Perspective*, Addison-Wesley, Reading, Mass, 1978.

Argyris, C., 'Teaching smart people how to learn', *Harvard Business Review*, May–June, 1991.

Argyris, C., *On Organizational Learning*, Blackwell, Cambridge, 1993.

Argyris, C., *Knowledge for Action*, Jossey-Bass, San Francisco, 1993.

Argyris, C. and Schon, D., *Theory in Practice: Increasing Professional Efficiency*, Addison-Wesley, Reading, Mass, 1974.

Barnard, C., *The Functions of the Executive*, Harvard University Press, Cambridge, Mass, 1938.

Barnard, C., *Organization and Management*, Harvard University Press, Cambridge, Mass, 1948.

Bartlett, C. and Ghoshal, S., *Managing Across Borders*, Harvard Business School Press, Boston, 1989.

Belbin, M., *Management Teams: Why they succeed or fail*, Butterworth Heinemann, Oxford, 1984.

Belbin, M., *Team Roles at Work*, Butterworth Heinemann, Oxford, 1993.

Belbin, M., *The Coming Shape of Organization*, Butterworth Heinemann, Oxford, 1996.

Bennis, W., *The Planning of Change* (with Benne, K.D. & Chin, R., 2nd edition), Holt, Rinehart & Winston 1970.

Bennis, W. and Nanus, N., *Leaders: The Strategies for Taking Charge*, Harper & Row, New York, 1985.

Bennis, W., *On Becoming a Leader*, Addison-Wesley, Reading, 1989.

Bennis, W., *Why Leaders Can't Lead*, Jossey-Bass, San Francisco, 1989.

Bennis, W., *An Invented Life: Reflections on Leadership and Change*, Addison-Wesley, Reading, 1993.

Bennis, W., *Organizing Genius: The Secrets of Creative Collaboration*, Addison-Wesley, Reading, Mass, 1997.

Binney, G. and Williams, C., *Leaning into the Future*, Nicholas Brealey, London, 1995.

Brech, E.F.L. (editor), *The Principles and Practice of Management*, Longman, London, 1953.

Burns, J.M., *Leadership*, Harper & Row, New York, 1978.

Byrne, J., 'Corporate anorexia: a lack-of-foresight saga', *Business Week*, 19 September, 1994.

Campbell, Andrew, 'The point is to raise the game', *Financial Times*, 14 September, 1994.

Campbell, A. and Koch, R., *Break Up!*, Capstone Publishing, Oxford, 1997.

Campbell, A. and Luchs, K.S., *Strategic Synergy*, Butterworth Heinemann, 1992.

Carnegie, D., *How to Win Friends and Influence People*, Simon & Schuster, New York, 1937.

Champy, J. and Hammer, M., *Reengineering the Corporation*, Harper Business, New York, 1993.

Champy, J., 'Time to reengineer the manager', *Financial Times*, 14 January 1994.

Champy, J., *Reengineering Management: The Mandate for New Leadership*, HarperBusiness, New York, 1995.

Chandler, A., *Strategy and Structure*, MIT Press, Boston, 1962.

Chandler, A., *The Visible Hand: The Managerial Revolution in American Business*, Harvard University Press, Cambridge, Mass, 1977.

Chandler, A., *Managerial Hierarchies* (with Deams, H., editors), Harvard University Press, Cambridge, 1980.

Chandler, A., *Scale and Scope: The Dynamics of Industrial Capitalism*, Harvard University Press, Cambridge, Mass, 1990.

Deming, W.E., *Quality, Productivity and Competitive Position*, MIT Centre for Advanced Engineering Study, MIT, Cambridge, Mass, 1982.

Deming, W.E., *Out of the Crisis*, MIT, Cambridge, Mass, 1982.

Drucker, P.F., *The New Society*, Heinemann, London, 1951.

Drucker, P.F., *The Practice of Management*, Harper & Row, New York, 1954.

Drucker, P.F., *Managing for Results*, Heinemann, London, 1964.

Drucker, P.F., *The Effective Executive*, Harper & Row, New York, 1967.

Drucker, P.F., *The Age of Discontinuity*, Heinemann, London, 1969.

Drucker, P.F., *Concept of the Corporation*, John Day, New York, 1972.

Drucker, P.F., *Management: Tasks, Responsibilities, Practices*, Harper & Row, New York, 1974.

Drucker, P.F., *Managing in Turbulent Times*, Harper & Row, New York, 1980.

Drucker, P.F., *Innovation and Entrepreneurship*, Heinemann, London, 1985.

Drucker, P.F., *The Frontiers of Management*, Heinemann, Oxford, 1987.

Drucker, P.F., *The New Realities*, Heinemann, London, 1989.

Drucker, P.F., *Managing the Nonprofit Organization*, Harper Collins, 1990.

Drucker, P.F., *Managing for the Future*, Butterworth Heinemann, Oxford, 1993.

Drucker, P.F., *Managing in Times of Great Change*, Butterworth Heinemann, Oxford, 1995.

Fayol, H., *General and Industrial Management*, Pitman, London, 1949.

Follett, M.P., *The New State: Group Organization – The Solution of Popular Government*, Longman, London, 1918.

Follett, M.P., *Creative Experience*, Longman, London, 1924.

Follett, M.P., *Freedom and Coordination*, Pitman, London, 1949.

Follett, M.P., *Dynamic Administration* (editors Fox, Elliot & Urwick, Lyndall), Harper & Row, New York, 1941.

Ford, H., *My Life and Work*, Doubleday, Page & Co, New York, 1923.

Goold, M., Campbell, A. and Alexander, M., *Corporate-Level Strategy*, John Wiley, New York, 1994.

Goold, M. and Campbell, A., *Strategies and Styles*, Blackwell, Oxford, 1987.

Goold, M. and Luchs, K.S., *Managing the Multibusiness Company*, Routledge, 1995.

Goold, M. with Quinn, J.J., *Strategic Control*, FT/Pitman, London, 1990.

Graham, P. (editor), *Mary Parker Follett: Prophet of Management*, Harvard Business School Press, Cambridge, Mass, 1994.

Hamel, G. and Heene, A. (editors), *Competence-Based Competition*, John Wiley, New York, 1995.

Hamel, G. and Prahalad, C.K., *Competing for the Future*, Harvard University Press, Cambridge, 1994.

Hammer, Michael, 'Reengineering work: don't automate, obliterate', *Harvard Business Review*, July–August 1990.

Hammer, M., *The Reengineering Revolution* (with Stanton, S.) HarperCollins, New York, 1995.

Handy, C., *Understanding Organizations*, Penguin Books, London, 1976.

Handy, C., *Gods of Management*, Business Books, London, 1978.

Handy, C., *The Future of Work*, Basil Blackwell, Oxford, 1984.

Handy, C., *The Making of Managers* (with John Constable), Longman, London, 1988.

Handy, C., *The Age of Unreason*, Business Books, London, 1989.

Handy, C., *Inside Organizations: 21 Ideas for Managers*, BBC Books, London, 1990.

Handy, C., *Waiting for the Mountain to Move and other reflections on life*, Arrow, London, 1991.

Handy, C., *The Empty Raincoat*, Hutchinson, London, 1994.

Handy, C., *Beyond Certainty: The changing world of organizations*, Century, London, 1995.

Heller, R., 'Fourteen points that the West ignores at its peril', *Management Today*, March 1994.

Herzberg, F., *The Motivation to Work* (with Mausner, B. and Snyderman, B.), Wiley, New York, 1959.

Jay, A., *Management and Machiavelli*, 1970.

Juran, J.M., *Quality Control Handbook*, McGraw-Hill, New York, 1951.

Juran, J.M., *Managerial Breakthrough*, McGraw Hill, New York, 1964.

Juran, J.M., *Juran on Planning for Quality*, Free Press, New York, 1988.

Kanter, R.M., *Men and Women of the Corporation*, Basic Books, New York, 1977.

Kanter, R.M., *The Change Masters*, Simon & Schuster, New York, 1983.

Kanter, R.M., *When Giants Learn to Dance*, Simon & Schuster, London, 1989.

Kanter, R.M., *The Challenge of Organizational Change* (with Stein, B. and Jick, T.D.), Free Press, New York, 1992.

Kanter, R.M., *World Class: Thriving locally in the global economy*, Simon & Schuster, New York, 1995.

Kotler, P., *Marketing Management: Analysis, Planning, Implementation and Control*, Prentice Hall, New Jersey, 1994 (8th edition).

Levitt, T., *Innovation in Marketing*, McGraw Hill, New York, 1962.

Levitt, T., *The Marketing Mode*, McGraw Hill, New York, 1969.

Levitt, T., *The Marketing Imagination*, Free Press, New York, 1983.

Levitt, T., *Thinking About Management*, Free Press, New York, 1991.

Lorenz, C., 'The very nuts and bolts of change', *Financial Times*, 22 June 1993.

Machiavelli, N., *The Prince*, Penguin, London, 1967.

McGregor, D., *The Human Side of Enterprise*, McGraw Hill, New York, 1960.

Maslow, A., *Motivation and Personality*, Harper & Row, New York, 1954.

Mintzberg, H., *The Nature of Managerial Work*, Harper & Row, New York, 1973.

Mintzberg, H., *The Structuring of Organizations*, Prentice-Hall, New Jersey, 1979.

Mintzberg, H., *Structures In Fives: Designing Effective Organizations*, Prentice-Hall, New Jersey, 1983. (This is an expurgated version of the above.)

Mintzberg, H., *Power In and Around Organizations*, Prentice Hall, New Jersey, 1983.

Mintzberg, H., *Mintzberg on Management: Inside Our Strange World of Organizations*, The Free Press, New York, 1989.

Mintzberg, H., *The Strategy Process: Concepts, Contexts, Cases* (with J.B. Quinn), 2nd edition, Prentice Hall, New Jersey, 1991.

Mintzberg, H., *The Rise and Fall of Strategic Planning*, Prentice Hall International, Hemel Hempstead, 1994.

Mintzberg, H., 'Musings on management', *Harvard Business Review*, July–August, 1996.

Morse, J. and Lorsch, J., 'Beyond Theory Y', *Harvard Business Review*, May–June, 1970.

Ohmae, K., *The Mind of the Strategist*, McGraw Hill, New York, 1982.

Ohmae, K., *Triad Power: The Coming Shape of Global Competition*, Free Press, New York, 1985.

Ohmae, K., *The Borderless World*, William Collins, London, 1990.

Ohmae, K. (editor), *The Evolving Global Economy*, Harvard Business School Press, Boston, 1995.

Ohmae, K., *The End of the Nation State*, Harper Collins, London, 1995.

Ouchi, W., *Theory Z*, Addison-Wesley, Reading, Mass, 1981.

Parkinson, C.N., *Parkinson's Law*, John Murray, London, 1958.

Pascale, R., *Managing on the Edge*, Simon & Schuster, New York, 1990.

Pascale, R. and Athos, A., *The Art of Japanese Management*, Penguin Books, London, 1981.

Peters, T., and Waterman, R., *In Search of Excellence*, Harper & Row, New York & London, 1982.

Peters, T., *A Passion for Excellence* (with Nancy Austin), Collins, London, 1985.

Peters, T., *Thriving on Chaos*, Macmillan, London, 1987.

Peters, T., *Liberation Management*, Alfred P. Knopf, New York, 1992.

Peters, T., 'Out of the ordinary', syndicated column, 23 July 1993.

Peters, T., 'In praise of the secular corporation', syndicated column, 26 March 1993.

Peters, T., *The Tom Peters Seminar*, Vintage Books, New York, 1994.

Peters, T., *The Pursuit of Wow!*, Vintage Books, New York, 1994.

Porter, M., *Competitive Strategy: Techniques for Analyzing Industries and Competitors*, Free Press, New York, 1980.

Porter, M., *Competitive Advantage: Creating and Sustaining Superior Performance*, Free Press, New York, 1985.

Porter, M., *Competition in Global Industries*, Harvard Business School Press, Cambridge, Mass, 1986.

Porter, M., *The Competitive Advantage of Nations*, Macmillan, London, 1990.

Prahalad, C.K. and Doz, Y., *The Multinational Mission: Balancing Local Responsiveness and Global Vision*, Free Press, London, 1987.

Rothbard, M., *Economic Thought Before Adam Smith and Classical Economics*, Edward Elgar, London, 1995.

Schein, E.H., *Process Consultation*, Addison-Wesley, Reading, Mass, 1969.

Schein, E.H., *Organizational Psychology* (3rd edition), Prentice Hall, Engelwood Cliffs, New Jersey, 1980.

Schein, E.H., *Organizational Culture and Leadership*, Jossey-Bass, San Francisco, 1985.

Schon, D., *Beyond the Stable State*, Random House, New York, 1978.

Semler, R., *Maverick!*, Century, London, 1993.

Senge, P., *The Fifth Discipline: The Art and Practice of the Learning Organization*, Doubleday, New York, 1990.

Senge, P., with Roberts, C., Ross, R., Smith, B., and Kleiner, A., *The Fifth Discipline Fieldbook: Strategies and Tools for*

Building a Learning Organization, Nicholas Brealey, London, 1994.

Sloan, A.P., *My Years with General Motors*, Doubleday, New York, 1963.

Smith, A., *The Wealth of Nations*, Modern Library, New York, 1937.

Stacey, R., *Complexity and Creativity in Organizations*, Berrett Koehler, San Francisco, 1996.

Taylor, F.W., *Shop Management*, Harper & Row, New York, 1903.

Taylor, F.W., *The Principles of Scientific Management*, Harper & Row, New York, 1911.

Toffler, A., *Future Shock*, Bodley Head, London, 1970.

Toffler, A., *The Third Wave*, Bantam, New York, 1980.

Townsend, R., *Up the Organization*, Michael Joseph, London, 1970.

Trompenaars, F., *Riding the Waves of Culture*, Nicholas Brealey, London, 1993.

Trompenaars, F., with Hampden-Turner, C., *The Seven Cultures of Capitalism*, Piatkus, London, 1994.

Tzu, Sun, *The Art of War* (trans. Griffith), Oxford University Press, Oxford, 1963.

Urwick, L. (editor), *The Golden Book of Management*, Newman Neamc, London, 1956.

Waterman, R., *The Renewal Factor*, Bantam, New York, 1987.

Waterman, R., *The Frontiers of Excellence*, Nicholas Brealey, London, 1994.

Watson Jr., T., *A Business and its Beliefs: The Ideas that Helped Build IBM*, McGraw Hill, New York, 1963.

Weber, M., *The Theory of Social and Economic Organization*, Free Press, New York, 1947.

Weber, M., *The Protestant Ethic and the Spirit of Capitalism*, Scribner's, New York, 1958.

INDEX